Soldiers, Saints & Sinners

Soldiers, Saints & Sinners

Stories of Long Ago

HARBERT ALEXANDER

*Illustrations by **Allison East***

Copyright 2015 by Harbert Alexander Sr.

All rights reserved. No part of this book may be reproduced or utilized in any form or by any means, electronic or mechanical, including photocopy, recording or by an information storage and retrieval system, without permission in writing from the publisher.

Library of Congress Cataloging-in-Publication Data

ISBN: 978-0-9963458-3-5

Printed and bound in the United States of America by Ingram Lightning Source.

First edition

Editing, layout, and design: Jacque Hillman
Illustrations: Allison East
Photography: Jesse Hillman
Cover: Jacque Hillman and Wanda Stanfill
Portrait of Harbert Alexander: Mitch Carter

To contact the author, write him at harbertalexander1@gmail.com

The HillHelen Group LLC. 124 E. Baltimore St. Ste. 118
Jackson, TN. 38301
www.jacquehillman.com   www.jessehillman.com

CONTENTS

Preface and Acknowledgments vii

Introduction ix

Chapter 1 The Holy Cheat. 1

Chapter 2 Early Settlers in Big Hatchie Country. 9

Chapter 3 Bombers Over Halls. 17

Chapter 4 Brothers-in-Law. 23

Chapter 5 Ghosts Around Us. 29

Chapter 6 The Lion Who Flew. 35

Chapter 7 Jackson's Grand Hotel. 41

Chapter 8 Old Times at the Ball Park. 49

Chapter 9 Football's Toughest Coach. 55

Chapter 10 Confederate Long Rifle. 61

Chapter 11 Tragedy in the Courthouse. 67

Chapter 12 Top Gun. 73

Chapter 13 The World's Largest Man.	79
Chapter 14 The Great Influenza Epidemic.	83
Chapter 15 Top Coaches.	89
Chapter 16. Albert the Drinking Duck.	95
Chapter 17. The Game Warden, Ray Henry.	101
Chapter 18. The Man Who Flew Around the World.	107
Chapter 19. The Music Men.	113
Chapter 20. The Family Tree.	121
Chapter 21. La Belle Village.	129
Chapter 22. Sweetheart of the Confederacy.	135
Chapter 23. The Waffle King.	139
Chapter 24. Buford.	145
Chapter 25. Christmas 1945.	151
Bibliography	156
About the Author	158

Preface and Acknowledgements

My thanks to all those who offered suggestions or helped me along the way. Fred Culp, Gibson County historian, introduced me to George Frederick Burgoyne Howard, the Holy Cheat. Lawrence Taylor led me on a tour of the courthouse where Judge Hu Anderson fell to his death. Mary Julia and Fred Gause of Brownsville led me to a ridge looking over Hatchie Bottoms near the little town of Orysa where the Williams family settled. Joe B. Guinn helped me with the location of old trails and riverboat landings along the Hatchie River.

Billy King, Denmark historian, introduced me to Joseph Merriwether, a young Confederate soldier, who marched away to war and never came back. Mrs. Stanley Allen of La Grange took me through her home, Westover of Woodstock, where Lucy Pickens, the Queen of the Confederacy, lived. Robert Reeves took me to Civil War sniper Jack Hinson's cave and gravesites. (He has two!)

Allison East made the stories come to life with her illustrations. Jacque Hillman, my editor, kept me on track, typing my manuscript, correcting my spelling, and making certain I met publishing guidelines.

As always, Nora, my wife and partner for more than fifty years, offered encouragement and advice and overlooked my piles of books and papers in every chair.

As I often say, "Our history is all around us, if we only look." There are many stories waiting to be told – help me find them.

Introduction

For more than half a century, I have been telling our story – the stories of people and events that create our history. In many ways, our history reminds me of a circus parade passing by, of people who lived or were born here.

Soldiers, Saints & Sinners follows the path of two of my previous books, *Tales of Madison* and *Old Trails and Tales of Tennessee*. Once again, go back in time with me and ride across West Tennessee in a covered wagon with the first settlers. Travel with me to La Belle Village, where time seems to stand still, or fly around the world with Steve Fossett, or climb into an airplane with Gilmore, a pet lion.

There are five Civil War stories: One tells the story of a young Confederate surgeon; one is about Lucy Pickens, "The Sweetheart of the Confederacy," and another is about a Confederate sniper on the Tennessee River.

Go to the New Southern Hotel when it was the center of downtown Jackson, or once again play with the toys of Tigrett Industries. As Christmas approaches, let your thoughts slip to the best of all holiday seasons, when the soldiers came home from the war in Europe in 1945.

The Holy Cheat was an 1880s British con man who posed as a Baptist minister.

Chapter One

The Holy Cheat

Perhaps you might have guessed that something was wrong when you first heard his name – George Frederick Burgoyne Howard.

An Englishman, he was a Baptist preacher – at least, he said he was. In 1883, a committee of the First Baptist Church in Jackson was formed to find a pastor to occupy their pulpit, the position then vacant. Dr. Howard accepted the call and preached his first sermon on September 11, 1883.

That he took Jackson by storm is no surprise. Years later, John A. Pitts, a prominent Tennessee attorney, described

Dr. Howard: "He was a most distinguished looking man, full fleshed and well proportioned, a blonde with long flowing beard and flaxen curly hair, both fine as silk, full grayish blue eyes and skin as fine textured and rosy as a girl's."

He dressed in the height of fashion and in good taste, and always wore gloves, a silk hat, Prince Albert coat, and white vest with black trousers. He walked with the slightly rolling gait of a sailor, but as elastic as if on springs. He was blessed with a splendid tenor voice, highly cultivated, and sang beautifully; he played the piano well and was a delightful conversationalist, well versed in history and the fine arts.

In the pulpit, he was dignified and eloquent with a smooth flow of words in pure English. Being unmarried, he was popular with the ladies and could be seen frequently riding around with his lady friends. With his fine voice and skill as a pianist, he soon became the life of the party wherever he was in attendance. An enthusiastic diner, he frequently said it took five meals a day of rich food to satisfy him!

And yet another side of Dr. Howard soon began to manifest itself. Church members began to notice that his sermons were lacking in thought or ideas. One member said he had a "diarrhea of words and a constipation of ideas." He was egotistical and criticized prominent church members for trivial matters such as their table manners. One of the first members to leave the church was Dr. Herman Hawkins who began attending services at St. Luke's Episcopal Church.

In the fall of his first year, Dr. Howard received permission for a leave of absence to visit his father in England. During the time he was gone, the deacons received just one postcard supposedly written just before he boarded ship.

While he was away, several leading members of the church, suspecting that Dr. Howard was an imposter, initiated a search into his prior life. The results were published in a leading Baptist newspaper, the Baptist and Reflector, with the following charges:

- His name was Howlett, not Howard.
- Rather than being a member of the aristocracy of England, he was the son of an obscure policeman.
- After enlisting as a sailor in a merchant ship, he deserted, joined another ship and ended up in South Carolina.
- His reputation in South Carolina was so bad he was run out of the state and ended up in Georgia working in a loan office and studying law.
- As his reputation followed him, he changed his name, professed religion and became a Baptist minister under the name of George Frederick Burgoyne Howard.

After a stormy meeting with the deacons, Howard denied all charges and resigned his pastorate. Following this, some fifty members resigned and organized a new church called Central Baptist on the northeast corner of Deaderick and Highland with Dr. Howard as their pastor.

Dr. Howard then engaged the law firm of Pitts and Hays and brought suit for $50,000 against the First Baptist deacons. As it was necessary to obtain records and sworn depositions from London, the law firm proposed to send their representative to accomplish this. Dr. Howard went ahead to gather witnesses and soon cabled back it would not be necessary to send someone as he could do this himself, which he did.

Upon his return, when the trial began, the depositions were challenged. Even though they seemed to be genuine, the handwriting was similar to that of Dr. Howard's! After this, attorneys resigned, and he was forced to defend himself. Nevertheless, the jury ruled in his favor and awarded him one cent! It had taken five years before the suit could be settled.

During this five-year period, Howard married and lived in Jackson on West Baltimore Street. As a pastor of his newly formed church, he published two Baptist papers, the True Baptist and the Fairview Advocate, though Jackson newspapers continued inflammatory articles about him.

Yet the intrigue around Dr. Howard continued as he embarked on a new career. Because of his English background, he was employed as an agent to go to London to promote American railroad securities to English investors. Shortly after his arrival in England, he sent back reports of marvelous success far beyond expectations. Yet mysterious delays seemed to hinder his progress until his employers cabled him to return to America to report on his progress, which he did. His reports to the railroad directors were so satisfactory, he was promoted to manager of the Gulf and Tennessee Railroad!

While things looked good in Tennessee, strange things were happening in London. During the period that Dr. Howard was in England, an individual named William Lord Moore of London sent soliciting letters to a large number of people in rural sections of the United States. These letters stated that while looking into the records, he found many large English estates that had not been settled because the rightful heirs had not been found. As the person to whom the letter was addressed had the same name as one of the heirs, he could obtain a large sum of money, but only if he sent four pounds ($20) to cover administrative expenses.

United States authorities received so many complaints that Scotland Yard in London was consulted. They found that William Lord Moore was the same person as Dr. Howard. A few weeks later, two United States revenue officers raided Dr. Howard's office in Jackson and shut it down. Dr. Howard, somehow learning of the raid, fled to Canada. Upon being assured he would receive a fair trial, he returned to Jackson to prepare his defense.

Three months later, in 1893, the trial was held in Jackson and was said to be the greatest criminal trial ever held by the government. Three members of Scotland Yard testified. Also present was the United States ambassador to England, the consul general to England, and Robert F. Lincoln, the former ambassador to England and the son of Abraham Lincoln.

After three weeks of testimony and deliberation, the jury found Dr. Howard guilty on all twenty counts and sentenced him to ten years confinement at the Federal Penitentiary in Columbus, Ohio.

Having served a portion of his sentence, Howard escaped and fled to Horton, Michigan, where he organized a church named The Ethical Society. He also became involved with two women at the same time and faced a damage suit. Up to his old tricks, he began a swindling scheme similar to the one he used in England. Upon his arrest and return to prison, he told the warden he was glad to be back!

He was released from prison in 1904 and returned to Jackson for a short period before leaving for New York and England.

Looking Back... Jackson's oldest church is First Presbyterian, organized in 1823. First United Methodist Church dates to 1826.

Provisions to sustain the settlers were purchased in Mobile, Alabama, enough to feed both family and servants for a year. In January 1824, the Williams family set forth. The journey lasted about two and a half months and covered 300 miles. Before departing, Mr. Williams went to North Carolina and had a large covered wagon made with leather curtains and sleeping quarters for the ladies.

Chapter Two

Early Settlers in Big Hatchie Country

One of the greatest stories of American history is that of Manifest Destiny, a widely held belief that American settlers were destined to expand throughout the continent, first in New England and finally all the way to California with the Gold Rush of 1849. It is commonly known as the "settling of America."

There were no white settlers in West Tennessee until the treaty with the Chickasaw Indians was signed in 1816. At first, only a few families arrived, but soon hundreds would follow. Some would remain in West Tennessee, but others would move on.

The first settlers, only a few, arrived in 1819 stopping east of Jackson near where Lake Graham is today. The little settlement was known as Cotton Gin Grove. The following year another group arrived and settled near the Forked Deer River. This location was named Alexandria, in honor of one of the group, Adam Rankin Alexander. These two settlements merged in 1822 to become Jackson.

Sometime in the 1820s, probably 1824, a family named Williams moved from their home in Mississippi and settled in the deep woods of the Hatchie River Bottoms. The story of that family is contained in a book, *Old Times in West Tennessee,* published by Joseph S. Williams in 1873. Long out of print, the book was reprinted recently by the University of Mississippi.

Describing the Williamses' trek from Mississippi is difficult because of the things we do not know. Joseph Williams was twelve years old when the trip began. He traveled with his family and servants but does not reveal their names. We know how long the trip took, but we do not know exactly where they departed from or where they settled. The biggest question, however, is why they left their home and moved into the depths of Hatchie Bottoms. The answer to this probably is land grants to Revolutionary War veterans.

These land grants came from the federal government as well

as from nine states. The size of the grants varied from 200 acres to as much as several thousand acres, depending on the person's rank and service. A similar system was in place for veterans of the War of 1812. (There are some two hundred grants to veterans of the Revolutionary War named Williams.)

The Williamses describe their former home as being in "the sands of the old settled part of Mississippi, south of latitude 32 degrees." From this, it seems they lived near the Gulf Coast. Based on migration patterns, I expect that they moved to Mississippi from either Virginia or North Carolina.

Provisions to sustain them were purchased in Mobile, Alabama, enough to feed both family and servants for a year. In January 1824, they set forth. The journey lasted about two and a half months and covered 300 miles. Before departing, Mr. Williams went to North Carolina and had a large covered wagon made with leather curtains and sleeping quarters for the ladies. With them were twenty milk cows and calves and twenty hogs. When they began the trip with the men either riding horses or walking behind the wagon, followed by the servants and animals, it was quite a parade.

On the fifth day they entered the Choctaw territory where they were well received and given venison and wild turkeys in exchange for trade goods. Though the Choctaws were helpful to the travelers, Williams described them as filthy and lazy.

Soon after leaving the Choctaws, they entered Chickasaw territory where once again, they received gifts and food. When the caravan arrived at the capital of the Chickasaw nation, they stopped for several days to rest and clean themselves and all of the animals. The chief of the Chickasaw nation soon came for a visit, accompanied by all of his Negro slaves. Though he was both intelligent and powerful, he was described as a "great mass of fat."

On the last day of February, they crossed into West Tennessee and reached Bolivar, forty days after leaving their home in Mississippi. Bolivar was a small trading post on the bank of the Hatchie River. It is known today as "Old Hatchie Town." Being mainly an Indian trading post, it had little to offer the travelers. Here they crossed the river, turned west and reached Denmark after several days. Little mention is made of Denmark other than finding a "three-notched" road, which had just been laid out connecting Denmark and Jackson.

The following afternoon, they reached Brownsville, which had just been laid out and established as the county seat of Haywood County. At that time, it had about a dozen houses and a log jail and courthouse. Continuing west toward Memphis, they reached their destination in the untouched wilderness of Hatchie Bottoms. I can only assume they had a map or document describing the property, its location and boundaries. Williams wrote that they did not have the use of a compass. They arrived at the site on the second week of March after a trip of forty-eight days.

By the end of March, a double log house had been completed and enough land cleared to grow a garden. Next, land was cleared to plant corn and a small area to plant cotton. To get this much done in such a short time period, there must have been a large number of slaves.

As the Williamses adapted to their new environment, they encountered some unfamiliar animals. As the days grew warmer and the humidity increased, a multitude of strange insects emerged. Mosquitoes, ticks, and red wasps led the way followed by spiders, deer flies, and a little insect called "no see-ums" that tended to crawl into your eyes and ears.

Though there was an abundance of deer and turkey, as well as small game such as squirrels and rabbits, there were other residents far more dangerous. Bears, wolves and panthers all lived in Hatchie Bottoms in the 1800s, though they are gone today. (A panther is similar to a mountain lion.) Throughout Williams' book, there are numerous encounters with bears and panthers. Bears, especially young ones, were edible. Roasted bear paws were a delicacy.

Soon after the Williamses arrived, there were many families

who followed, settling into counties around them. Other families followed them into the "Big Hatchie" country, but the Williamses were the first. West Tennessee would continue to grow and change into what we know today. And yet much of Hatchie Bottoms remains just as it was in the 1830s. The bears, wolves, and panthers are long gone, but the rest of the wildlife is just as it was. There is no other place like it.

On a spring morning, walk into the big woods. Be still and listen to the sounds around you and imagine what it was like 190 years ago when the Williams family first arrived.

Looking Back... Two of America's most notorious criminals have come through Jackson. "Machine Gun" Kelly was arrested here in 1922 and spent sixty days in jail. Al Capone came through Jackson in 1947 on an Illinois Central train, in his coffin.

Daniel Boone traveled through West Tennessee in 1776. A beech tree with his name carved on it still stands north of Jackson near Oakfield.

The first Native American nomadic hunters came through West Tennessee more than nine thousand years ago, and continued to live and hunt in here until the first settlers arrived in 1819. We have been here less than two hundred years by comparison.

The B-17 was a four-engine heavy bomber aircraft developed in the 1930s for the United States Army Air Corps. It was primarily employed in daylight precision bombing of German industrial and military targets. The B-17 dropped more bombs than any other military aircraft in World War II.

Chapter Three

Bombers Over Halls

The Japanese attack on Pearl Harbor on Sunday morning, December 7, 1941, marked the beginning of World War II for the United States.

As America began to mobilize its war efforts, Congressman Joe Cooper began promoting Dyersburg, Tennessee, as a site for an Army air base. In early 1942, the War Department began to show interest in locating the base in Halls, Tennessee, in Lauderdale County. Area newspapers reported the presence of Army survey teams at the end of March, and by the second week in April, the first offers for land purchases were opened. Because of Congressman Cooper, the new site was named the Dyersburg Army Air Base, even though it was located in nearby Halls.

Approximately 2,400 acres of land was leased by the War Department. What had once been fields of cotton and sharecropper homes was now an Army base! More than seventy families were displaced and had to find new homes. Construction began in late May. Construction of the runways began in September. Barracks, administration buildings and maintenance facilities soon followed. Three long 6,167-foot runways were constructed in a triangle along with parking ramps and taxiways. By the summer of 1943, the base consisted of more than 300 buildings. Although the barracks were sufficient for the soldiers, there was nothing available for wives, mothers, and children who wanted to be with their airmen before they went into combat. Families in nearby Dyersburg, Ripley, Brownsville, and Halls transformed attics, garages, and sleeping areas to help out.

The Dyersburg Army Air Base was the largest combat aircraft training base built during the early phase of World War II. It was the only inland B-17 Flying Fortress training base east of the Mississippi River. Between 7,000 and 8,000 airmen were trained to fly. A crew for a B-17 aircraft consisted of ten people, including a pilot, co-pilot, navigation specialist (who manned cheek guns when under attack), radio operator, bombardier, flight engineer (who manned the top turret) and four remaining gunners who covered the ball turret, left waist gun, right waist gun and tail gun. Each crew had four officers and six enlisted men. Training in Halls lasted eighteen weeks for each crew. It was designed to be their final training phase.

The first B-17 to land was commanded by Brigadier General Nathan Bedford Forrest, great-grandson of the Confederate general. (He would not survive the war.) The B-17 was a four-engine heavy bomber aircraft developed in the 1930s for the United States Army Air Corps. It was primarily employed in daylight precision bombing of German industrial and military targets. It was a high-flying, long-range bomber that was able to defend itself and return home despite damage it had received. The B-17 dropped more bombs than any other military aircraft in World War II.

With average ages between eighteen and twenty-three for the crew, their instructors didn't have an easy task in teaching how to fly the big aircraft, nor did the crew find it easy to learn. Training flights were all over the Mid-South to the Gulf Coast. Fifteen planes crashed, and 114 lives were lost. The first crash was on May 1, 1943, at the base. Two months later on July 12 was the next crash near the Mississippi River.

Shortly thereafter, two gunners were accidentally ejected from their plane while flying over Covington and did not survive. Thereafter, all aircraft crews were required to wear parachutes. Other planes crashed at Cape Girardeau, Missouri; the Kentucky line near Latham, Tennessee; Baton Rouge, Louisiana; Tunica, Mississippi; and, in Tennessee, Forked Deer, Lake Lauderdale, Owl City, Covington, and Roellen, proving you didn't have to go to Germany to become a fatality!

One tenant sharecropper was accidentally killed when a training crew, practicing gunnery, strafed his house in the Mississippi River bottoms. Even today, seventy years later, shell casings can still be found in the fields along the Mississippi River.

When the war in Europe ended in May 1945, the Dyersburg base was out of a job. The strategic bombers were no longer needed, and training completely stopped in August 1945 when Japan surrendered. On September 1, 1945, the base was placed on standby. Despite efforts to keep the base in Halls, demobilization began quickly. The base was closed and quickly dismantled. The land was sold and buildings were either torn down or sold. Even the former morgue was moved and at one point became the Halls mayor's residence. Just as quickly as the Army had come, it departed in the same manner.

Today there is little trace of Dyersburg Army Air Base. The former north-south runway is used as a runway for the local Halls Airport, now named Arnold Field. The Dyersburg Army Air Base Museum, now the Veterans Museum, is in a building on the former aircraft parking apron.

Looking Back... In 1858, a professor from Spring Creek named Isham Walker applied for a patent for an airplane. The machine was named the "Giant Trout." Congress turned down his request. If Walker had been successful, he would have been 45 years ahead of the Wright Brothers.

In February 1945, two hundred German prisoners of war were barracked at McKellar Field in Jackson. Many of them picked cotton and peaches and were paid $25 a month. By March 1946, the prisoners began their trip home to Europe.

In 1837, President Martin Van Buren appointed Robert J. Chester as the United States Marshal in the Western District of Tennessee. In 1870 and 1872, he was elected to the Tennessee Legislature.

Chapter 4

The Brothers-in-Law

In Jackson's early days, Dr. William Edward Butler and Robert Johnson Chester were two of its leading citizens. They were like actors with leading roles, center stage in a play that was just beginning. They came to Jackson at different times and from different locations. The one thing they had in common was they both were born in Carlisle, Pennsylvania, about 150 miles from Pittsburg.

Dr. Butler was born in 1790, the son of Colonel Thomas Butler, a veteran of the American Revolution and one of the three men who negotiated a treaty whereby the Cherokee

Indians agreed to sell their land to the United States. After graduating from the University of Pennsylvania, Dr. Butler moved to Murfreesboro.

During the War of 1812, Dr. Butler joined the staff of Colonel Thomas Hart Benton of the Second Regiment of Infantry and was present with them at the Battle of New Orleans, serving as Andrew Jackson's surgeon general. Following the war of 1812, Butler was with Jackson in two campaigns against the Creek Indians.

Following the treaty with the Chickasaw Indians in 1818, Butler accompanied James Caruthers on a trip down the Forked Deer River to Jackson in 1819, making him one of the first white people to come into West Tennessee. (The first settlers would arrive that year, settling just east of where Lake Graham is located today.)

Robert J. Chester was three and a half years younger than Dr. Butler. Because of confusion of the spelling of his middle name, he changed the J to I becoming Robert I. Chester. When he was a child, the family moved to Jonesboro where they owned the Chester Hotel, a frequent stopping place for Andrew Jackson and Sam Houston. During the War of 1812, Chester served as quartermaster under Generals Jackson and Winchester in Mobile, Alabama. Years later, when asked about his time as a soldier, he remembered how poor the

Army food was. The beef they were issued was rancid and full of worms. Before eating it, they would throw it against a tree. If it stayed there, they would eat it. If it started crawling up the tree, they left it alone!

When the war ended, he settled down in Carthage as a merchant and farmer. While there, he was appointed as a postmaster and also as a federal land grant surveyor. In 1824, he moved to Jackson and established himself as a merchant.

Dr. Butler and Robert Chester were brothers-in-law in that they both married nieces of Andrew Jackson. Butler married (Patsy) Martha Thompson Hays in 1813. It was not until 1825 that Robert Chester married Elizabeth Hays. Two of Robert's brothers also married Hays sisters. (One might wonder how many sisters there were!)

The two men were similar in some ways but different in others. Chester, who was single at the time, followed other travelers down wagon trails to Jackson. Butler loaded his family and all of their belongings on flat-keel boats, floating down the Cumberland to the Ohio River to the Mississippi and then poled their way up river on the Forked Deer (then called Okeena) to Jackson.

Though Dr. Butler had a medical practice in Murfreesboro, he never practiced medicine in Jackson, where he found too many things to do. In 1821, he planted his first crop of cotton and erected a cotton gin he had brought from Davidson County. The following year Butler and two associates donated thirty acres of land along with twenty-four acres they purchased from Thomas Shannon to establish the site of downtown Jackson. Besides his activities in getting Jackson started, Dr. Butler was Jackson's first banker, served on the first jury of the Circuit Court, farmer, land agent and Justice of the Peace.

Besides helping to facilitate the beginning of Jackson, Dr. Butler is best known for the 1823 race for a place on the state legislature against David Crockett, billed as "wealthy aristocrat versus the Bear Hunter." In his autobiography, Crockett said, "The doctor was a clever fellow, and I have often said he was the most talented man I ever run against for any office." (Crockett won, and Butler never again ran for office.)

Dr. Butler led a long and colorful life in Jackson, involved in everything around him. He died in 1882 at the age of 93. Dr. H.E. Hawkins, a Jackson physician, remembered Butler as being stubby, heavyset, extremely deaf, one who walked with a cane and had a big booming voice. It is said that Dr. Butler sat in his front yard on Royal Street with a heavy shawl around his shoulders. Famous for his profanity, he damned the weather if it was hot or cold.

Robert Chester continued as a merchant in Jackson from

1824 to 1835, also serving as United States postmaster for Jackson and Madison County. In 1825, he married Elizabeth Hayes, a marriage that produced six children before she died in 1841. In 1835, he moved to Texas and was commissioned as a colonel in the Texas Revolutionary Army, returning to Jackson the following year.

For two periods, Chester practiced law in Jackson. In 1837, President Martin Van Buren appointed Chester as the United States Marshal in the Western District of Tennessee. In 1870 and 1872, he was elected to the Tennessee Legislature to represent Gibson, Carroll, Henry and Madison counties.

In 1879, Chester County was created and named for him. Chester Street in Jackson is also named for him. Colonel Robert I. Chester died in January 1892, at the age of ninety-nine. At the time of his death, he was the oldest affiliating Mason in the United States. At his death, it was said, "The Great State of Tennessee had no better citizen."

Looking Back... When Andrew Jackson visited here in 1840, a huge ashcake weighing 120 pounds was cooked for the occasion. It took more than a bushel of meal to make the cake.

Tennessee was the 16th state to join the Union in 1796. The name Tennessee comes from a Cherokee village named Tanasie. The lonely pioneer with a flintlock rifle and a coonskin cap is a symbol of Tennessee's past.

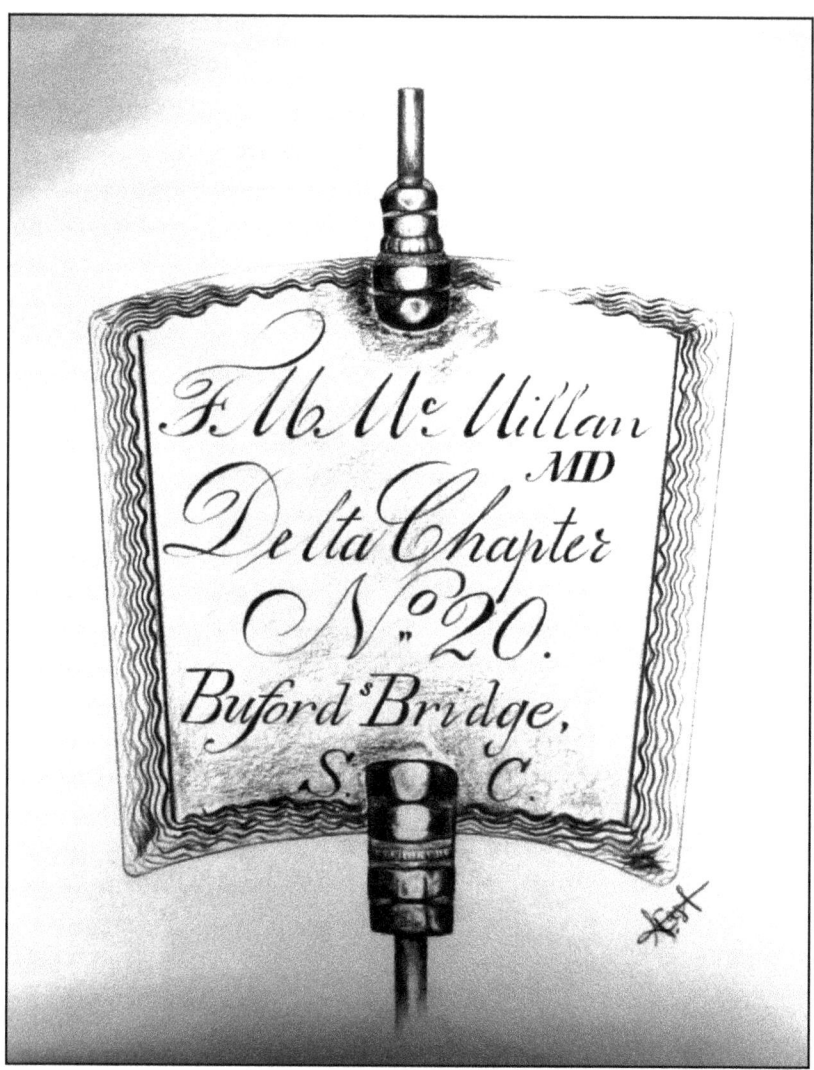

When the Civil War broke out, Dr. Frances McMillan joined the 25th Mississippi Infantry as a third lieutenant and assistant surgeon. Shiloh was the first battle the young surgeon would see.

Chapter Five

Ghosts Around Us

Not long ago, while walking along a field in Haywood County, I found an arrowhead.

It looked as if it had been made last week, rather than 2,000 years ago. How did it get there? Was it dropped or perhaps lost on a hunting trip? What was the man like who made that arrowhead? How I wish I could talk to him and ask him about his family, his food, and a hundred other things. Questions without answers.

From time to time, people doing yard work in Jackson along Highland Avenue or Royal Street will find a button or a lead bullet that was lost by Yankee soldiers when they occupied Jackson during the Civil War. Old letters and records speak of the lines of canvas tents with the thousands of soldiers camped here. I wish I could talk to them and ask them why they are here, are they homesick, and what do they think of this little Southern town. But like the Indians, they are long gone, even though I feel their presence when I find an arrowhead or Civil War bullet. They are like ghosts.

By an odd set of circumstances, the story of one Confederate soldier came back to life. It was a story of a young Confederate doctor who died nearly 150 years ago. The story began when a man with a metal detector found a small gold watch fob with a name and a Masonic symbol on it. It was found near Chewalla, Tennessee, a small town of less than 200 persons on the Memphis and Charleston railroad. In October 1862, Confederate General Earl Van Dorn and his army of 22,000 soldiers marched through Chewalla en route to Corinth, Mississippi. Following the Battle of Corinth, a defeated Confederate army retreated back through Chewalla with Union soldiers closing in on them from two directions.

The watch fob had a Masonic emblem on one side and F.M. McMillan, M.D. Delta Chapter No. 20 Buford's Bridge, S.C., on the other. Several months after it was found, I purchased it from a dealer in Civil War artifacts. But the story of who Dr. F.M. McMillan was and how the watch fob got to Chewalla remained a mystery. No South Carolina troops fought in West Tennessee and Buford's Bridge, South Carolina, no longer seemed to exist. Despairing of ever finding out about Dr. McMillan, I put the watch fob away and forgot about it.

Several years later, I saw an ad in a magazine about a lady in Virginia who did research on Civil War soldiers. I called her and told her about the watch fob. Several hours later, she called back and said, "I think I have your soldier. Meet Dr. Frances McMillan, Confederate surgeon!"

I had been looking in the wrong direction. It never occurred to me to look in Mississippi. I felt like I had found an old friend. Frances Marion McMillan, nicknamed "Barney," was born in 1837 near Colston, South Carolina. He was one of eight boys and seven girls, and six of the boys became Confederate soldiers.

After graduating from the Medical College of New York, Dr. McMillan traveled through Europe for a time before setting up his medical practice in Mississippi. When the Civil War broke out, he joined the 25th Mississippi Infantry as a third lieutenant and assistant surgeon.

Shiloh was the first battle the young surgeon would see. With 3,000 dead and more than 16,000 wounded, surgeons on both sides were overwhelmed. In many ways, it was just the beginning. In a letter dated September 16, he wrote, "The scenes of that day are vivid in my imagination even now. Confederate and Federal soldiers lay scattered over the field distinguished by their gray and blue uniforms. Thousands of thrown away rifles and a few cannon were lying there. These and the thousands of dead and wounded soldiers made up a scene of dread magnificence."

On the night of October 3, 1862, the Confederate Army camped at Chewalla, preparing to attack Corinth. On October 4 and 5, following the withdrawal from Corinth, the weary army again camped in the fields and along the roadside of Chewalla. There can be little question that this was when Dr. McMillan lost his Masonic watch fob.

By August 1863, he was a brigade surgeon with the 42nd Tennessee infantry with the rank of major and participated in all of the battles of the Atlanta Campaign. As the war began to enter its final stages, the 42nd Tennessee was nearly annihilated at the Battle of Franklin. The brigade commander was twice wounded before being captured. All of the staff officers were killed, as was the color bearer. The highest-ranking officer left was a captain. There were only one hundred men left when General John Bell Hood's army moved on to attack Nashville. Dr. McMillan was left behind to care for the wounded. There is no further record of Dr. McMillan. It seemed I had come to the end of the story, but there was another chapter with a surprise ending.

In a book titled "A Faithful Heart: The Journal of Emmala Reed 1865-1866," reference is made to Dr. McMillan having been a prisoner at Camp Chase in Columbus, Ohio. Conditions were brutal there with a high mortality rate. Apparently he had been captured shortly after Franklin and was a prisoner for about six months. The journal describes Dr. McMillan as follows: "So moral and good, a Brigade Surgeon in Johnston's Army and now I wonder if he is broken down completely and not thirty yet." When he returned home, he lived just two years, dying of rheumatic fever in 1868.

At last, the story of Frances Marion McMillan and the gold watch fob seemed to be complete. But one last part of the story remained unfinished. I wondered if I could find any of his descendants. After months of frustration, a friend gave me the name of a man in Bamberg, South Carolina. When I called him, a rich South Carolina accent said, "Sir, you are talking about my great-uncle!" Several months later, I drove to Bamberg to visit the grave of Frances Marion McMillan and return the watch fob. Though he had been dead for more than 140 years, the discovery of a long-lost relic brought him back to life for a family in South Carolina and for me.

On April 13, 1930, Gilmore, the lion cub, went for his first plane ride. To satisfy criticism from the Humane Society, Gilmore was outfitted with his own parachute.

Chapter Six

The Lion Who Flew

At first, the little lion cub had no name. He was a real lion, an African lion, even though he had been born at a lion farm in Agura, California. But the real story is about the man who came to California to buy him and who flew all over America in an airplane.

The pilot was Roscoe Turner, the most famous aviator and master showman of the 1920's and 1930's, the Golden Age of Aviation.

Roscoe was born nine miles west of Corinth, Mississippi, in 1885 in a small house, sometimes described as a shack on the family farm. As part of a hard-working, deeply Christian family, it was expected that one day he, too, would be a farmer. When he finished the 10th grade (all the school had to offer) he turned to other things than plowing the land.

Fascinated by the speed of trains coming and going through Corinth, he dreamed of being a locomotive engineer. Frustrated by his father's insistence that he become a farmer or work in a bank, he ran away to Memphis when he was sixteen where he worked in a grocery store and drove a truck delivering ice. When World War I broke out, Roscoe enlisted in hopes of being trained as a pilot but ended up as an ambulance driver. In 1918, he was accepted into a program as a Flying Cadet, training to be a balloon pilot and parachutist. In 1919 he mustered out of the army with the rank of lieutenant.

In 1919, Roscoe and a partner formed the Roscoe Turner Flying Circus, and for five years they toured the Southeast taking passengers on "joyriding" flights and performing stunts that included wing-walking and mock airplane crashes. For a period, he decorated his plane as a flying cigar. Later he used the plane to host teas for society ladies and to make radio broadcasts. In 1928, Roscoe began working for Howard Hughes as a pilot in the movie *Hell's Angels*.

In 1928, he began air racing in a plane sponsored by Shell

Oil Company. The following year, he attempted to set a new transcontinental speed record but failed to do so.

Always striking in his appearance, Roscoe wore a self-designed uniform during all of his flying years, highlighted with a pair of wings designed by a jeweler, a beige officer-type cap, sky-blue tunic, cavalry-type jodhpurs, and polished riding boots. Deeply tanned, he grew a pencil-thin mustache and waxed it so it could be twisted to needle-like ends. And yet, despite his appearance and growing fame, Roscoe's life and career took an abrupt turn when he bought a lion cub.

Acting on impulse one day when he saw a lion's head on a road sign advertising Gilmore Lion Head Motor Oil and Red Lion Gasoline, he decided to buy a lion and take him on a record-setting flight.

On February 7, 1930, a cub had been born on a lion farm in Agura, California, and the cub could be purchased for $200. Though Roscoe didn't have that much money, he persuaded the owner to donate the lion for the publicity it would bring for his business. Promptly named Gilmore, the lion was to become as much a part of Roscoe's image as his waxed mustache and fancy uniform.

When Gilmore was purchased, he weighed seventeen pounds. Roscoe put him on a leash and took him everywhere he went in Los Angeles. Gilmore seemed to have no aversion to dogs and cats, but they were unsure of him. When Roscoe took Gilmore on the golf course, everyone wanted to pet him.

On April 13, 1930, Gilmore went for his first plane ride. Calm at first, he became terrified and jumped into Roscoe's lap. It would be several months before Gilmore was comfortable in the air. To satisfy criticism from the Humane Society, Gilmore was outfitted with his own parachute.

Gilmore stayed in hotels with Roscoe and went to fancy restaurants. The lion's appearance proved to be a trademark that even Roscoe had not expected. Later Roscoe predicted, "When I'm gone, I'll be remembered as the guy who flew with a lion." Gilmore flew over 25,000 miles with Roscoe, establishing or breaking a number of speed records. Gilmore soon became known as "The Flying Lion."

When Gilmore reached 150 pounds, it was the end of the partnership. Gilmore was too big for the plane, and in 1940, Gilmore was placed at an African lion farm where Roscoe paid for his food. Years later a friend asked Roscoe why he continued to pay for Gilmore's food. Roscoe replied, "For a long time, he paid my bills; now it's my turn." When Roscoe visited him in 1948, after an eight-year absence, it was predicted Gilmore would not know Roscoe, but the big lion, weighing 600 pounds, let out a roar and placed a paw on Roscoe's arm.

Gilmore died in 1952 at the age of twenty-two and a half. His body was preserved, and he now resides in the National Air and Space Museum at the Smithsonian in Washington. Roscoe Turner died in June 1970 in Indianapolis. When the National Air and Space Museum opened in 1976, Roscoe's trophies were placed on exhibit. His Boeing 247 was suspended from the ceiling and standing beneath it is Gilmore, the Flying Lion!

Looking Back... Highland Park was an amusement center from the Gay Nineties and early 20th Century. Located between Crescent and Westwood Avenue, it had a baseball park, roller coaster and ice skating rink.

What Jackson business operated downtown at 200 Dr. Martin Luther King Jr. before the post office was there? It had quite a role in Jackson's downtown folklore!

When the May 4, 2003, tornado hit the New Southern and all of downtown Jackson, rather than a disaster, it presented an opportunity to return the lobby and second floor with its Gold Room to the way it looked when it opened in 1924.

Chapter Seven

Jackson's Grand Hotel

At first there was a bank there, long before a hotel. In August 1822, fifty-four acres were surveyed and divided into 104 lots. This was to become the city of Jackson and was a compromise between two small settlements. One was Cotton Gin Grove, east of Jackson near today's Lake Graham. The other was Alexandria near the Forked Deer River just west of Jackson. Within a week, all of the lots were sold. The more expensive lots were the ones closest to the courthouse in the center of town. James Greer, a government surveyor, bought one of the best lots across the street (East Baltimore) from the site where the courthouse was to be built.

In August 1835, Greer sold the lot to the Union Bank of Tennessee. The bank occupied the site for twenty-five years until the onset of the Civil War when the bank failed. Not much is known or remembered about the bank, except for one event that occurred on the night of February 3, 1859.

George C. Miller, who served as the bank clerk, lived in an apartment at the rear of the bank. That night someone persuaded him to open the bank vault and then struck him in the back of the head with a hammer which fractured his skull and killed him. The killer took $17,300 in paper notes and $5,700 in gold coins. The killer was never found. However, on September 12, 1985, city workers uncovered a cache of gold coins while preparing a new parking lot on West Main Street. All of the coins were dated prior to 1860 and totaled the same amount of money stolen from the bank. Who placed them there and why he never returned for them will forever remain a mystery.

Jackson was occupied by Union soldiers in mid-1862. They would remain for a year. The building where the Union Bank had been located was used as a headquarters for Colonel Marsh of the 11th Illinois Cavalry. In 1866, the Bank of Madison was chartered and thus became the second bank to occupy the site. (This bank later moved to the northwest corner of Market and Lafayette Street, where it failed in 1890.)

Ben Gates ran a boarding house after the bank moved. In 1870 W.D. Robinson ran the boarding house, followed in 1874 by Mrs. Mary L. Trimmier, who called it "The Trimmier House." What had been called a hotel, but in reality was little more than a boarding house, was transformed into a more modern structure when Captain and Mrs. James E. Bright bought the property. Under their ownership, it soon became a popular destination for travelers. Mrs. Bright sat at the head of the table and entertained her guests, not only with her charm but with her menus. In 1880, part of the old wooden structure was replaced with brick.

In 1887, Mrs. J.H. Day purchased the hotel. Prior to the purchase, Mrs. Day had run a boarding house on property where the Jackson Sun would later be located. After she took possession, she rebuilt and enlarged the building and renamed it the Southern Hotel. In the thirty years she owned the hotel, it grew and became popular throughout the Southeast. Mrs. Day died in April 1919. The heirs then leased the hotel to H.L. Hodge who operated it until A.D. Noe and Son of Hopkinsville, Kentucky, purchased it in 1924, and immediately began dismantling much of the old structure and rebuilding. By January 1928, the project was complete. The hotel was now eight stories high with 220 rooms and a new name – The New Southern Hotel. A formal opening was held on January 5, and the hotel was ready for what lay ahead.

For the next forty years, the downtown area was the heart of Jackson, and the New Southern was the place to be. Many wedding receptions, dances, and parties were held there, and many brides threw their garters to the hopeful bridesmaids on the steps below.

Because of its location, the hotel was a natural spot for politicians seeking election. Lyndon Baines Johnson spoke on a platform in front of the hotel in 1960 when he was campaigning for the vice- presidency on a Democratic ticket with then-Senator John F. Kennedy of Massachusetts. That same year, Governor Buford Ellington hosted a luncheon for former President Harry Truman, who was soliciting votes for the Democratic ticket. In 1966, Richard Nixon climbed onto a makeshift bell stand to speak in the lobby when rain forced him inside.

The coffee shop, located on the ground floor, was a center of activity for hotel guests as well as people who worked downtown. Look at the Christmas menu: appetizer, soup, choice of nine entrees, two vegetables, and dessert for only one dollar! No wonder it was popular!

The success of the New Southern was a product of the times.

There were no motels and not many hotels. Downtown Jackson had no competition. There was no U.S. 45 Bypass, no malls, and the railroads brought people into and out of Jackson every day. Today, according to the phone book, there are twenty-three hotels and motels!

In addition to The New Southern, the Noe family owned other hotels in Tennessee, Kentucky, and Alabama, including The Owensboro; The New Central in Hopkinsville, Kentucky; The Dixie Carlton in Birmingham, Alabama; and The Read House in Chattanooga, Tennessee.

Not only people but birds and other animals were sometimes guests or residents. The inhabitants were parakeets, canaries, and a dwarf parrot owned by Miss Ruby Mann, a resident of the hotel who was also an employee. The birds were housed in an aviary nine feet square equipped with a birdbath, mirrors, a trapeze, balls, bells, and lights. Perhaps the most unusual guest to register at the hotel was a horse! In 1948, as part of a promotion to sell savings bonds, the horse checked into the hotel with his handler. He made the front page in the evening Jackson Sun with a pencil in his mouth at the front desk checking in!

A.D. Noe Jr. died in 1947, and his son Albert Noe III took over management of the hotels until his death in 1965. In 1967, Morris Crocker purchased the hotel and ran it as a hotel, office building, and apartment complex for the next 25 years. His son, Hal Crocker, inherited the property. When the May 4, 2003, tornado hit the building and all of downtown Jackson, rather than a disaster, it presented an opportunity to return the lobby and second floor with its Gold Room to the way it looked when it opened in 1924.

Times have changed for the New Southern as Jackson and its downtown have changed. It will never again be the center of Jackson as it once was. But in a different way in a different time, the future looks bright ahead.

Looking Back... Jackson was originally named Alexandria in honor of Adam Rankin Alexander, one of the first settlers. Another Tennessee town was named Alexandria, so the name was changed to honor Andrew Jackson, our seventh president.

The first laws of Jackson were passed in 1823. They included fines for running a horse in town ($20), shooting a pistol in town ($20) and a fine of $5 for fastening matches to dogs' tails.

Christmas - 1940
Served from 11:30 A.M. to 9:00 P.M.

CHOICE
    Fresh Gulf Shrimp Cocktail   Fresh Baltimore Oyster Cocktail
    Cherry Cup   Half Grapefruit, Maraschino   Relish Platter

CHOICE
    Cream of Asparagus, Argenteuil   Garden Vegetable Soup
    Hot Tomato Bouillon

ENTREE
    Grilled Whole Speckled Trout, Montpellier Butter
    Poached Filet of English Sole, Normandy
    Fresh Mushroom and Chicken Liver Omelette
    Baked Kentucky Ham, Glazed, Champagne Sauce
    Grilled Steak of Spring Lamb, Vert Pre, Mint Sauce
    The Christmas Turkey, Chestnut Dressing, Cranberry Sauce
    Broiled Mignon of Beef on Toast, Arlington
    Unjointed Spring Chicken, Southern, Corn Fritter
    Roast Choice Prime Rib of Beef, Au Jus

CHOOSE TWO
    Fresh Cauliflower, Hollandaise   Lima Beans, Hoteliere
    Fresh June Peas, Bonne Femme   Fresh Brussel Sprouts
    Special Stuffed Baked Potatoes   Sultana Sweet Potatoes

CHOICE
    Holiday Salad
    Heart of Lettuce, Choice of Dressing

CHOICE OF DESSERTS
    Ambrosia and Fruit Cake   Boiled Custard   Mince Meat Pie
    Pumpkin Pie   Mint Parfait   Jello
    Ice Cream   Sherbet
    Demi Tasse
    Mints

$1.00 Per Cover

NEW SOUTHERN HOTEL — JACKSON, TENNESSEE

In 1926 and 1927, the Toledo Mud Hens of the Class AA American Association used Jackson as a spring training base for their preseason workouts. Casey Stengel was the manager. In later years, Stengel would be remembered as the beloved manager of the New York Yankees.

Chapter Eight

Old Times at the Ball Park

Not long ago while I was watching a baseball game at The Ballpark at Jackson, my thoughts drifted back more than sixty years to a much earlier Jackson Generals team.

A new ball park, an old racetrack at the West Tennessee State Fairgrounds, had been converted into a baseball diamond. The old grandstand with 4,000 seats was more than adequate for seating and a new scoreboard and lights were added. Not only could they play games at night, a new ordinance now allowed Sunday afternoon games. The franchise had been purchased from the Clarksville Colts in the

Kitty League (Kentucky, Illinois, and Tennessee).

As young boys, we would go down and pester the coaches and players into letting us be batboys, which we frequently did. We were always in need of baseballs, and we often received balls as our pay. We learned a lot of new words from the players, words we didn't repeat at home. Gabby Stewart, a former major league player with the New York Giants, was player-manager. Our favorite player was Maurice (Maury) Partain, who stole eighty-three bases that year. As we grew older, we would go to Memphis in the spring before the season started when the major league teams would come through. They stayed at The Peabody Hotel, where we would ask for autographs and request to be batboy. This worked like a charm, and we were able to sit in the dugout with the Chicago Cubs, Chicago White Sox, and St. Louis Cardinals. I rode to the park sitting in Eddie Stanky's lap and sat on the bench with Stan Musial and the other Cardinals. Small wonder that I am a baseball fan!

Baseball in Jackson began more than 150 years ago when West Tennessee College (now Union University) had a team. Jackson had its first professional team in 1903 when the Red Railroaders joined the Kitty League. By year's end, the name had changed to Red Ravens. Though they had a good season, the team withdrew its franchise at the end of the year.

Eight years later a group of fans enticed the Harrisburg, Illinois Miners to move to Jackson. For the second time, Jackson had a team in the Kitty League. Because the team was already in next-to-last place, the name was changed to the Climbers, in hopes they would climb in the standings. The team failed to do so and folded at the end of the season.

The Jackson Athletic Association acquired the city's third Kitty League franchise in 1924. This time the team was named the Blue Jays because their new uniforms had a big blue "J" on them. The low point of the season came on a Sunday afternoon in Mayfield, Kentucky, when the entire team was arrested for violating a city ordinance of playing baseball on Sundays!

For the third time, the Kitty League folded at the end of the 1924 season. Jackson and the Dyersburg Forked Deers then joined the newly formed Tri-State League. Midway in the second season, the league folded due to financial problems. Once again, Jackson was left without a baseball team.

In 1926 and 1927, the Toledo Mud Hens of the Class AA American Association used Jackson as a spring training base for their preseason workouts. Casey Stengel was the manager. In later years, Stengel would be remembered as the beloved manager of the New York Yankees. One of his best quotes was: "If we are going to win the pennant, we've got to start thinking we're not as smart as we think we are!"

He is the only man to lead his team to five consecutive World Series championships. He is still considered to be one of the best managers of all time. He was elected to the Baseball Hall of Fame in 1966.

In April 1937, manager John McGraw brought his National League team to Jackson to play the Mud Hens. More than 4,000 people packed the stands to see the Giants, who had five future Hall of Famers on the team, including McGraw.

In 1935, the Kitty League started once again under the ownership of Hartle Gilland who named the team the Jackson Generals. Games were played in Lakeview Park where the Bemis Square is located today. The league folded in 1942 as Americans turned their attention to the prospect of war in Europe and in the Pacific. On a happy note, a group of major league players played an exhibition game on October 17 against a local team. Among the players were Joe Garagiola, playing third base wearing a gorilla mask, and Yogi Berra.

Baseball began again in Jackson in 1950. City officials converted the racetrack into a baseball diamond with a new fence and scoreboard and named it Municipal Park. The Generals played there until 1954, when the team folded after losing twenty-six straight games! It would be forty-four years before professional baseball would return to Jackson with the

Diamond Jaxx and Pringles Park, now the Jackson Generals and The Ballpark at Jackson.

Jackson has had professional baseball for more than a hundred years. Of all of the teams, and all of the players, one player stands above the rest. His name is Ellis Kinder. Born in Atkins, Arkansas, his nickname was "Old Folks," perhaps because he was thirty-one years old when he made his debut with the St. Louis Browns. He spent three years with the Jackson Generals from 1939 to 1941. He played twelve years in the major leagues before retiring in 1957. Always ready to have fun, his off-field antics were as memorable as his pitching performances. In one of the most unusual occurrences in baseball, a seagull flew over Fenway Park in Boston and dropped a three-pound fish on Kinder's head while he was pitching. Kinder continued to live in Jackson. He was only fifty-four when he died after undergoing open-heart surgery.

Looking Back... Robert Cartmell, a Civil War soldier and farmer from Jackson, kept a diary for 65 years. It is our best record of life in Jackson during the Civil War.

The Southern Engine and Boiler Works was once the largest business in Jackson. From 1922 to 1926, it made Marathon automobiles, the first automobile manufactured in the South.

Coach Robert Victor Sullivan is often called the toughest football coach of all time. His name is listed as Bob "Bull" Sullivan or "Cyclone" Sullivan. At other times, he was known as "Big Bob" or "Shotgun."

Chapter Nine

Football's Toughest Coach

Paul "Bear" Bryant is generally considered to be one of the toughest coaches in the history of college football. Much of this legend is based on the year he became head coach at Texas A&M University. On the first of September, he took one hundred players to Junction, Texas, a small hill country town.

Temperatures averaged one hundred degrees or better in a period of no rain. Practices lasted from first light to dark with no water breaks allowed. Over 70 percent of the group quit before the ten-day camp was over. The movie *Junction Boys* was based on this camp. Could there be a tougher football coach than Bryant? Perhaps there was!

Coach Robert Victor Sullivan is often called the toughest football coach of all time. His name is listed as Bob "Bull" Sullivan or "Cyclone" Sullivan. At other times, he was known as "Big Bob" or "Shotgun." Bear Bryant is recorded as saying he wasn't nearly as tough as Bull Cyclone Sullivan!

Bull, one of six children, was born in Echola in Tuscaloosa County, Alabama, in 1918. The family was desperately poor. When his father died of a heart attack, his mother supported the family by working in a cotton mill in Aliceville, Alabama near the Mississippi state line. When the family moved, he stayed behind to play football at Aliceville High School where he captained the team and was its biggest and best player. After graduation, having been offered a football scholarship, Bull entered Union University.

In 1942, Union was a football powerhouse, going undefeated and outscoring the competition 211-75. Bull was the center on the team, and was good enough to receive an offer to play professional football with the Detroit Lions. Instead, he joined the Marine Corps and reported to Parris Island as America moved toward World War II. The members of the 1942 football team vowed to come back and finish school together after the war. When Bull returned to Union in 1945, he found that Union had eliminated the football program. At the end of the school year, he transferred to the University of Nevada, where he played football and was a standout as a center and linebacker on the football team.

After completing his time in Nevada, he returned to Scooba, Mississippi, where he became football coach at East Mississippi Junior College, now called East Mississippi Community College, throughout most of the 1950s and 1960s. Scooba had only 734 inhabitants with roughly 256 to 360 young people (with a third of them girls). Nearly every boy in Scooba played football for Bull. However, many of them quit, unable to accept his harsh discipline.

The year before his arrival, Scooba had lost every game they played and had done so for many years. To show his toughness, Sullivan scheduled their first game with Little Rock Junior College, the 1949 junior college champion of America. Scooba won 34-14, and the legend had begun to grow with the team winning eight games and only losing three. In his first three years, the team won twenty-one games which was more victories than the team had won since the school was chartered in 1927.

Bull was so mean no one dared to hire him as a college or professional coach. Norm Van Brocklin, head coach of the Atlanta Falcons, once tried to hire him to coach the Falcons' offense. Bull replied, "Why, Norm? Why would I come up there and work for you, when I already know more football than you do!" Bull designed the players' uniforms with skull and crossbones on the helmets and short-sleeved black trim jerseys with five stars across the chest. He was the last coach of his time to give up leather helmets.

Most frightening was his physical presence. He was big all over with ham hock arms, huge fists and a melon-sized head. When one of his players decided to quit the team, he snuck out at night so as not to face Bull.

His temper on the field during a game was without parallel, tearing his coat off and stomping on his hat and screaming at the players and officials. One game he became so angry that he stormed onto the field and kicked the game ball thirty yards through the goalposts. On another occasion, he yelled so loudly that one of his players crawled under the bench the players were sitting on.

Practice under Bull was often brutal with four-hour sessions in the morning and again in the afternoon. One of the best-remembered techniques was to have his defensive players line up on the edge of a pond and then have the offense charge them. One of the players remembered how many pairs of football cleats were lost in the mud of that pond.

Many of Coach Turner's players quit the team. One player

quit six times, but kept coming back. His players hated him, but ended up loving him. One former player remembered, "Bull would do anything to you, but then he would do anything for you."

Bull could out-think other coaches. He was years ahead of his time in developing a passing game when other teams passed the ball only as a last resort. With limited resources, he created winners out of losers and men out of boys. Perhaps he was the toughest coach of all time, but he was one of the best.

Looking Back... One of the earliest books written by a Jackson author was "Wise Sayings of Wise Men." W.A. Caldwell, president of the First National Bank of Jackson, was the author. It was written in 1944 and published by McCowat-Mercer Press of Jackson.

Thomas Edison, commonly known as the greatest inventor in history, was here briefly in the latter part of 1865 working as a telegraph operator.

Jack Hinson, a man of peace, began a campaign of revenge after his sons were caught hunting on their own land, accused of being Confederate spies, and beheaded.

Chapter Ten

Confederate Long Rifle

It was a big gun. Beautifully made by master craftsmen, it was no ordinary gun. Far too heavy to be a hunting rifle, it was never designed to kill a deer or a turkey. Its purpose was very different. It was made to kill a man, a specific individual, and later other men. The gun, and the individual who shot it, became very efficient at killing Union soldiers, and in so doing, created a legend unlike any other in the blood-soaked history of the Civil War.

For Jack Hinson, life before the Civil War was not only pleasant but prosperous. A native of North Carolina, Hinson moved to Tennessee about 1830. Hinson, fifty-seven, was already old by the standards of the day when the Civil War broke out. He was only five feet five inches in height, but lean and strong, with unusually long arms, which led one lady to say many years later, "He looked like Popeye."

By 1850 Jack and his wife Elizabeth settled in Bubbling Springs with eight of their ten children. Bubbling Springs sat in a grassy valley about three miles southwest of Dover on 1,200 acres of land. Surrounded by family and servants, Jack and Elizabeth passed comfortably into middle age. Relatively isolated, the Hinsons led a tranquil life that would soon end as the nation moved toward conflict.

In November 1861, Union gunboats began shelling Fort Heiman in nearby Kentucky. For Bubbling Springs, only seven miles away, the reality of war could no longer be ignored. Three months later in February, following the Confederate surrender of Fort Donelson, Union occupation became a grim reality. At first, life for the Hinsons at Bubbling Springs continued as it did before the war. Because Jack Hinson was known as a man of peace and had befriended General Ulysses S. Grant, Union troops for the time being left them alone. That summer Hinson, aware of the turmoil around them, began the process of freeing his slaves, giving them the option of staying on as paid laborers.

Following an almost normal autumn, two of Jack's sons, George and his younger brother John, were arrested and charged as Confederate spies by a patrol of the 5th Iowa Cavalry. The boys were hunting on their own land. With no way to defend themselves against the charges, they were tied to trees and executed. After cutting the boys' heads off, the Union soldiers took the bodies were taken to Dover for display. According to local legend, the boys' heads were taken to the Hinson home and impaled on gateposts in the front yard. These killings, senseless as they were, set in motion the revenge that would follow.

The first step in avenging the killings was to obtain a gun that would kill a man at long range. Jack's choice was a .50 caliber rifle with a maple stock. Such a gun could not be obtained locally and would take some time to obtain, but Jack was in no hurry. While waiting for the gun, Jack began studying the patterns of Union patrols and the occupying force at Dover. To further avoid suspicion, Jack took the oath of allegiance to the United States in February 1863. The new gun weighed eighteen pounds and fired a conical-shaped minie ball. After weeks of testing the gun for accuracy, he was ready for the next step and ambushed a Yankee patrol, killing the lieutenant in charge. It was the same officer who had been responsible for the execution of Jack's boys. A few days later Jack struck again, when he ambushed a second Union patrol and killed the Union soldier who had impaled his sons' heads on the Hinson gateposts.

As rumors of his involvement in the two murders began to circulate, it became obvious that life at Bubbling Springs would soon end. Shortly after he moved his family to safety in Henry County, Union soldiers burned Jack's house and outbuildings. Looking for a temporary home, Jack settled into a cave high on a bluff overlooking the Tennessee River near the mouth of Leatherwood Creek. Below him stretched a narrow section of the river known as the Towhead Chute. (This was long before the Tennessee Valley Authority and the wide channel of today.) Any Union boat traveling through the chute would be a sitting duck for at least forty-five minutes. In the days that followed, Jack resumed his war against the Union. Choosing to shoot only officers, he began his work. Using a hammer and punch, he inscribed a tiny circle on the rifle barrel for each kill. There were thirty-six circles when the war was finally over.

In late summer 1864, Jack made military history when he attacked a naval transport boat loaded with soldiers and supplies. With multiple targets available, he killed all of the officers. The ship's captain then attempted to surrender the boat. With no way to take possession of his prize, Jack slipped away into the woods.

When the war finally ended in 1865, Jack's one-man war against the Union ended, and it was time to return to his family. Despite rumors of federal prosecution, Jack lived for twelve more years, dying in 1874.

Today the legend of Jack Hinson and his one-man war continues to grow. The spring still bubbles at the old homeplace, but there is no sign of the house. Jack's cave is accessible only by climbing up a steep bluff. Except for the monuments at nearby Fort Donelson at Dover, there is little trace of the war along the river. But one visible reminder of Jack Hinson remains. His long rifle is in a private collection, but if you are ever lucky enough to see it, look at the tiny circles on the barrel and think of the lives that were lost because of it.

Looking Back... The 6th Tennessee Regiment (CS) was from West Tennessee and trained at Camp Beauregard on Airways. Their first battle was Shiloh where they lost five hundred men. Of the twelve hundred men who marched away from Jackson in 1861, less than one hundred returned home from 1865.

Nathan Bedford Forrest was in West Tennessee twice during the Civil War. His first campaign was in 1862 which ended in December at the Battle of Parker's Crossroads near Lexington. He was back again the following year to gather men and supplies where he barely escaped by crossing the Hatchie River at Estanaula Landing.

Judge Hu Anderson was appointed to serve as presiding judge, Military Tribunal III in Nuremberg, Germany, by President Harry Truman. On trial were Alfried Krupp Von Bohlen and eleven other officials of the Krupp Armament Industry who were charged with the war crimes of active participation in arming Germany and using slave labor as workers.

Chapter Eleven

Tragedy in the Courthouse

Hugh Crump Anderson was born in McNairy County in 1851. He served two times as mayor of Jackson as well as city attorney and president of Peoples Savings Bank, prior to its failure. He died in 1915 while serving as speaker of the state Senate. His son Hu Carmack Anderson was born in 1890. Educated at Jackson High School, he received his law degree from Cumberland Law School. After graduation, he practiced law in Jackson before being called into service as a member of the 324th Field Signal Battalion during World War I.

Following the war, Anderson returned to private practice with the firm of McCorry and Anderson and later the firm of Anderson, Rothrock, and Carroll. At the death of Benjamin J. Howard, he became the attorney general for the 12th Judicial Circuit from 1917 to 1922.

In 1926, he formed a partnership with Sue White, the first female attorney to practice law in Jackson. White, a native of Chester County, earned a law degree from Washington College of Law in 1923. Prior to this, she worked in the women's suffrage movement. White achieved national notoriety for participating in a demonstration in which the National Women's Party burned an effigy of President Woodrow Wilson. For this, she was arrested and put in jail for five days.

After the Nineteenth Amendment was approved, "Miss Sue," as she was known, was appointed as clerk and later secretary for Senator Kenneth McKellar. Senator McKellar served as a United States representative from 1911 to 1917 and as a United States senator from 1917 to 1953.

Appointed to the Tennessee Court of Appeals in 1933, Judge Anderson was elected without opposition in 1934, 1942 and 1950. His work was interrupted when he was appointed to serve as presiding judge, Military Tribunal III in Nuremberg, Germany, by President Harry Truman. On trial were Alfried

Krupp Von Bohlen and eleven other officials of the Krupp Armament Industry who were charged with the war crimes of active participation in arming Germany and using slave labor as workers. Eleven of the twelve defendants were found guilty.

Upon completion of the trial, Judge Anderson returned to Jackson and resumed his position as presiding judge of the Tennessee Court of Appeals. On May 5, 1953, Judge Anderson arrived at the courthouse in Jackson where his office was located on the third floor. Each morning, he would take an elevator to the third floor as he usually arrived before the elevator operator, Miss Margaret McNeil.

On that Tuesday morning, however, Miss McNeil had arrived earlier than usual and had already taken attorney Whit LaFon to the third floor. Not knowing this, and assuming the elevator was on the first floor as usual, Judge Anderson unlocked the door and stepped into the dark elevator shaft, falling about twenty feet to the basement floor.

When Miss McNeil attempted to return the elevator to the first floor, it stopped, indicating that the door on the first floor was open. Returning to the third floor, she told Attorney LaFon of the problem. In response to calls, Judge Anderson replied he had fallen down the shaft and asked for help.

With people frantically trying to extricate Judge Anderson from the small space at the bottom of the shaft, it soon became evident that no one could reach him. Building custodian Virgil Taylor then sent a car to Whitehall School to pick up his twelve-year-old son Lawrence. After taking off his shirt, Lawrence was able to climb over the elevator motor and reach Judge Anderson. After determining that he was still breathing, Lawrence tied a rope around Judge Anderson so he could be pulled up the shaft to the first floor. Smith Funeral Home responded to the call and carried the judge to Webb Williamson Hospital on North Royal Street. At that time, the funeral home provided ambulance service.

In a front page story in the afternoon edition of the *Jackson Sun*, Sheriff E.O. Bruce was quoted as saying, "Judge Anderson stepped into the dark elevator shaft, thinking that the elevator was there, but the light was off." Doctors at the hospital said, "He was suffering from a fractured left leg above the knee, lacerations of the scalp and chin, probably a fracture of the lower jaw, and possible fracture of the skull." Two days later, Judge Anderson died of injuries from the fall. He was sixty-two years old. Members of the Tennessee Supreme Court, the Court of Appeals and the Bar of Tennessee served as pallbearers, and Judge Anderson was buried in Hollywood Cemetery.

Whenever I step onto an elevator, I often think of Judge Anderson and the elevator that wasn't there.

Herb Parsons shot trap with Clark Gable and Roy Rogers and duck hunted with Andy Devine. In the movie *Winchester '73*, he did the trick shooting for Jimmy Stewart.

Chapter Twelve

Top Gun

Though sixty hunting seasons have come and gone, memories of a long ago dove hunt are as clear as if it were yesterday.

My father and I had been invited to a hunt on a farm just west of town. It was opening day.

The season opened at noon, but before the hunt, lunch was served on long tables under giant oak trees. Ladies stood by the tables to make sure we filled our plates with fried chicken, pork barbecue and homemade cakes and pies.

There were dozens of hunters at the picnic tables, but one

table was set aside for the younger hunters. A pleasant middle-aged man came to our table and said, "Boys, I'm Herb Parsons and I'd like to eat lunch with you!" It was a unique experience to hear him talk about being a professional shooter for Winchester and about bear hunting in Alaska.

Several days later I returned to that farm with a friend for another dove hunt. But we arrived a little late, and most of the places around the field were already taken. One place, however, had two men and two ladies sitting side-by-side. It was a large area, and it seemed unlikely they could cover all of it, so we set up behind them. Moments later, four doves flew over, and they killed them all. As we watched, doves continued to come their way, but they never missed, and we never got a shot. We soon moved!

Later we found out that the four hunters were Herb Parsons and his wife and Lynn Binford and his wife from nearby Nutbush. Binford was considered by many to be as good a shot as Parsons. I often wondered if hunting would be as much fun if you never missed!

Herb Parsons was born in May 1908 on a rural West Tennessee farm in Fayette County. At first, he attended a one-room schoolhouse until the family moved to nearby Somerville where the family ran a boarding house. Always athletic, Herb played football and excelled at throwing the shot put on the track team. After graduating from Fayette County High School, he worked several years for a local wholesale grocery company.

When he was seventeen, he met Adolph Topperwein, Winchester's exhibition shooter. Topperwein and his wife Elizabeth, called "Plinky," were a team for forty years, traveling across the United States promoting Winchester. One of their favorite tricks was for Plinky to shoot a cigarette out of her husband's mouth or the buttons off his vest. Meeting Topperwein changed his life, and Parsons dedicated his life to mastering the sport of shooting for an audience. Shooting became an obsession.

In 1929, Winchester hired him as a field representative and salesman. His territory was the entire state of Mississippi, but his big break came several years later when Topperwein's vision began to fail, and Parsons was chosen to succeed him. After spending time developing his routine, he became Winchester's exhibition shooter.

In the 1940s, he gave 238 exhibitions to soldiers at military bases, and when the war broke out, he served as a gunnery instructor. When the war was over, he hit the circuit for Winchester, putting on thousands of exhibitions. He was the best modern goodwill ambassador the gun industry could have.

Parsons rose above all the celebrity shooters before him,

going back to Annie Oakley. He possessed a flair for the spectacular, a gift of gab, and most of all, he broke targets. An exhibition would last for fifty-seven minutes in which time he would fire 700 rounds of ammunition from numerous high powered rifles, shotguns and pistols.

Among his many tricks was hand-throwing seven clay targets into the air and breaking each one before they hit the ground. This was done with a Winchester Model 12. pump gun. Shooting a .22 rifle, he would throw a handful of washers into the air, shooting all of them, but pretending to miss one. He would then say, "I must of shot that one through the hole." He would then take a postage stamp and cover the hole. He would then shoot through the washer, destroying the stamp. Bending over, he would assume the position of a center on a football team. Throwing a handful of eggs through his legs, he would spin around and turn them into scrambled eggs.

Parsons performed in every state in the union. (There were only forty-eight states at the time of his death.) In 1946, he performed before 120,000 people at the World's Roundup in Cheyenne, Wyoming. As his fans grew, so did his circle of friends. He shot trap with Clark Gable and Roy Rogers and duck hunted with Andy Devine. In the movie *Winchester '73*, he did the trick shooting for Jimmy Stewart. At the height of his career, Winchester was booking him three years in advance.

More than anything, Herb Parsons was a hunter. Twice he won the National Duck Calling Championship in 1950 and 1951, and the international championship in 1949 and 1950. His saying was renowned: "Take your boy hunting and you won't have to hunt for him tomorrow."

In July 1959, Parsons underwent surgery for a hiatal hernia. A blood clot developed, and he died a short time later. At the pinnacle of his career, he was only fifty-one. In years to come, other shooters will emerge, but it is unlikely any will surpass Herb Parsons. Many people still remember him as the greatest shooter who ever lived!

Looking Back... Monroe Dunaway Anderson was once a bank teller in Jackson. Today he is best known as the man who founded the Anderson Cancer Center in Houston, Texas.

Tom Gaston was Jackson's most famous police chief. He was shot so many times, a Memphis newspaper simply reported, "Gaston shot again."

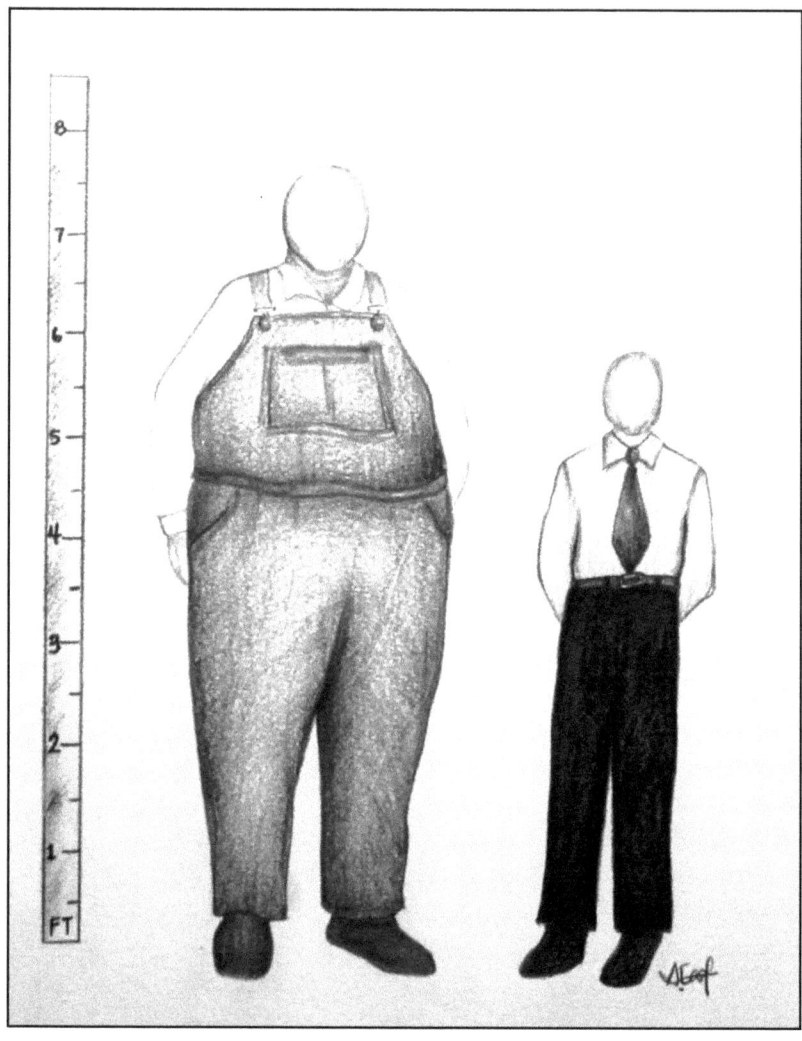

A giant of a man, Miles Darden was seven feet-six inches in height. At the end of age forty-six, he weighed 871 pounds but continued to grow. His weight was estimated to be 1,080 pounds when he died.

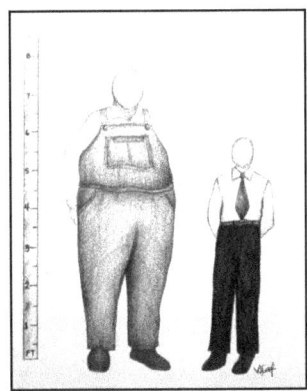

Chapter Thirteen

The World's Largest Man

Do you ever have a biscuit for breakfast? Could you have eaten two or perhaps more?

Miles Darden, once considered the largest man on earth, would eat forty biscuits, a pound of butter, two and half pounds of bacon, eighteen eggs and three quarts of coffee for breakfast!

Darden was born in Northampton, North Carolina in 1799. Sometime between 1827 and 1830, he moved to Tennessee. The 1830 census shows him as a resident of Madison County. By 1840, he was listed as a resident of Henderson County where he lived until his death in 1857.

A giant of a man, he was seven feet-six inches in height. At the end of age forty-six, he weighed 871 pounds but continued to grow. His weight was estimated to be 1,080 pounds when he died. In an amazing contrast, his wife Mary was only four feet eleven inches tall and weighed ninety-eight pounds! Darden's size was probably caused by a glandular deficiency, a malfunction of the pituitary gland.

At first he worked as a farmer, but in 1850, he opened a tavern and inn on the Lexington court square. Whenever he went anywhere, he rode in a wagon pulled by either two horses or two oxen. A staunch Baptist, when he attended church, he would lie on a blanket near the pulpit with a prayer book in his hand. (This was after he had broken several benches.) Perhaps the best known story about Darden's size is of three men, each weighing 200 pounds or more, who put on one of his coats, and with all of them in it, walked around the court square in Lexington.

His death in 1857 was apparently caused by rolls of fat around his neck that caused him to strangle. At the time of his death, his waist was six feet four inches. His coffin was eight feet long and required seventeen men to get him into it. A wall of the house had to be torn down to move him. Today, he sleeps peacefully in the Miles Darden Cemetery near the little community that is named for him about eight miles southwest of Lexington.

At the time of his death, he was described as the world's largest man. The Guinness Book of World Records, however, lists thirteen individuals who weighed more. Jon Brower Minoch of Bainbridge Island, Washington, is the heaviest, weighing 1,400 pounds. Minoch also holds the record for the greatest weight loss, losing 923 pounds! The next time you reach for another biscuit or piece of bread, remember Miles Darden!

Looking Back... Casey Jones was a railroad engineer from Jackson. Immortalized in a ballad, he is best remembered for his train wreck near Vaughn, Mississippi on April 30, 1900.

Bill Clinton is the only U.S. President to visit Jackson when he was still in office. He came here on August 19, 1996 along with Vice-President Al Gore.

The influenza epidemic in 1918 killed millions of people.

Chapter Fourteen

The Great Influenza Epidemic of 1918

In recent months, fears of an Ebola epidemic have filled the newspapers. Epidemics are nothing new.

Since the arrival of the Pilgrims, there have been nine epidemics of measles. Epidemics of cholera and smallpox have taken their toll. Before influenza, the yellow fever epidemics of 1873 and 1878 were the greatest disasters for West Tennessee and Mississippi.

Very few people remember or know about the influenza epidemic of 1918 unless their parents or grandparents told them. Perhaps it is overlooked because World War I had just ended, and American soldiers were beginning to return from battlefields in Europe. Perhaps it has been forgotten or ignored because people were tired of stories of those who had been killed or wounded and would not be coming home.

Unlike other diseases prevalent with the weak, elderly, or very young, the influenza epidemic killed millions of healthy adults. In Tennessee, the virus was most deadly in cities such as Nashville and Memphis. In one Middle Tennessee community of 500 people, 98 percent of them fell sick.

The war was over. It was not a time for sadness and death. And yet the epidemic was horrible. In the Midwest, where many think the influenza epidemic was born, it was the coldest winter in history. Over the next year, it flourished, killing more than a hundred million people. It killed more people in twenty-four weeks than AIDs has killed in twenty-four years. In some ways, it was reminiscent of the Middle Ages where victims turned black and blue, and priests in the world's most modern cities drove horse-drawn carts down the streets calling for people to bring out their dead.

The disease struck Nashville on the first of October. Within a few hours, the city hospital was overflowing with a number of patients listed as critical. By October 8, city schools were shut down. Five days later, all Nashville churches stopped holding services. The journal of the Tennessee Medical Association lists 435 people who died in Nashville. At the peak of the crisis, Nashville reported 10,000 to 15,000 cases, 7,000 in Chattanooga and 1,500 in Knoxville. The Banner in Nashville reported at one point that Memphis had a greater mortality rate than any other city.

Though sources in Jackson are scarce, newspaper stories give a glimpse of the severity of the epidemic. On November 11, the Great Lakes Naval Band, set to give a concert at the courthouse, had canceled their concert. Five days later, the Red Cross asked for all who could to send sheets, pillows, and nightgowns for distribution to those who were sick or in need.

Star Laundry had a message for its customers: "On account of sickness among our employees, seventeen girls on the sick list, we are handicapped to give the prompt service that we wish to do to meet the demands of the situation."

Though there were no quick cures, there was one unlikely candidate that stepped up. It was Vicks Vaporub! An advertisement stated: "The influenza germs attack the lining of the air passages. When Vaporub is applied over throat and chest, the medicated vapor loosens the phlegm, opens the air passages and stimulates the mucous membrane to throw off the germs."

Apparently, it worked as demand for the product soared. On November 11, the Vick Chemical Company asked druggists to conserve stock. Three million jars had already been shipped. Sales increased from $900,000 to $2.9 million in 1918!

On November 8, Dr. Frank Hamilton of the Madison County health department reported that 188 people died from influenza. Of that number, two of them serve as reminders of how tragic and sad the late fall of 1918 really was. After eight days of influenza, C.J. Austin died of pneumonia. He was forty-five years old. His son Jesse died several days earlier. When it was found that his father was at the point of death, his funeral was postponed. They were buried together in one large common grave in Hollywood Cemetery.

As the Christmas season approached, influenza, for the most part, began to disappear. It has been almost a hundred years since that terrible fall of 1918. It is painful to remember times like that, but tombstones across West Tennessee remind us of the time that influenza was here.

Nearly everyone who was alive in 1918 lost a friend or family member. Nearly a century after it occurred, medical historians are still unsure what caused the outbreak.

Looking Back... Yellow fever struck hard in West Tennessee in 1873 and again five years later. In 1878, 90 percent of the white population in Memphis contracted the disease and 70 percent of them died. In 1881, it was discovered that mosquitoes carried the disease.

Following Wallace Wade's two years at Vanderbilt, he was hired as head coach at the University of Alabama. Over the next seven years, Alabama won three national championships. In 1925 Alabama was undefeated and defeated Washington in the Rose Bowl.

Chapter Fifteen

Top coaches

Paul Bryant, the eleventh of twelve children of Wilson and Kilgore Bryant, was born in Moro Bottom, Arkansas. He was nicknamed "Bear" when he offered to wrestle a bear in a carnival when he was thirteen years old. That nickname would be with him throughout his life, and in many ways replaced his first name.

Following high school, he accepted a football scholarship at the University of Alabama where he played for four years. Following graduation in 1936, he was selected in the 4th- round of the draft by the Brooklyn Dodgers to play professional football, but chose to pursue a coaching career instead.

His first job was as an assistant coach at Union University in Jackson, Tennessee. Union had a football team from 1893 to 1952. Bear and his wife Mary Harmon lived in an apartment over a garage at 423 North Highland on property owned by H.L. Rice. Older Jacksonians have fond memories of the Bryants, especially how tenacious a bridge player Bear was.

When he was offered a position of assistant coach at Alabama, he returned to his alma mater. Over the next forty-six years, he served as head coach at Maryland, Kentucky, Texas A&M and Alabama. In the twenty-five years he coached at Alabama, the Crimson Tide won six national championships and thirteen Southeastern Conference titles. In 1981 when Alabama beat Auburn, he surpassed the all-time record for wins as a head coach.

Bear Bryant coached for a short time when he was here in 1936, but it is still fun to connect him with West Tennessee. Yet few people realize that Alabama had another great coach from West Tennessee. His name was Wallace Wade.

Wallace was born in Trenton, Tennessee in 1892. He was born and raised on a farm, and after thirty-two years of coaching, he retired as a cattle farmer. Five months after he was born, the University of Alabama played its first football game. Four years earlier in 1888, Duke University, then called Trinity College, played its first football game. The little boy from Gibson County, Tennessee would one day lead both of those teams to national prominence.

One of nine children, Wallace worked on the family farm when he wasn't in school. At the turn of the century, Trenton was a major grower and shipper of strawberries throughout the Southeast. One of his friends remarked that Wallace liked to work harder than anyone he ever knew. He first played football at Peabody High School in Trenton. Following high school, he attended Brown University where he played guard on the football team that went to the Rose Bowl in 1916.

After graduating from college, Wallace was hired as an assistant football coach at Vanderbilt University and as head coach of the basketball and tennis team. In the two years he was in Nashville, the football team was undefeated!

Following his two years at Vanderbilt, he was hired as head coach at the University of Alabama. Over the next seven years, Alabama won three national championships. In 1925 Alabama was undefeated and defeated Washington in the Rose Bowl. This was the first time a Southern Conference (now Southeastern Conference or SEC) had won the Rose Bowl. That game is commonly referred to as "the game that changed the South."

After his third national championship in 1930, Wade shocked the football world by resigning at Alabama and accepting the head coaching position at Duke University. In the sixteen years he coached at Duke, his teams won 116 games with only thirty-six losses and seven ties. His 1938 team was not scored on until losing to the University of California 7-3 in the Rose Bowl.

In later life, Wade was commissioner of the Southern Conference (now SEC) from 1951 to 1960. In 1955, he was inducted into the College Football Hall of Fame. In 1967, Duke's football stadium was renamed Wallace Wade Stadium in his honor. In 2006, a bronze statue of him was erected outside Alabama's Bryant-Denny Stadium alongside statues of Frank Thomas, Bear Bryant, Gene Stallings and now Nick Saban, the other head coaches who led Alabama to national championships.

As each fall season arrives, it will be football time in Tennessee. And as in most years, Alabama will most likely be a pre-season pick to win the national championship. And as part of that tradition of football excellence, remember two head coaches who had ties to West Tennessee.

Looking Back... Billy Graham preached in Jackson on June 15, 1951 before a capacity crowd of five thousand people at Rothrock Stadium (then part of Union University).

Albert the Drinking Duck was one of the most successful toys of all time. In a book about the famous scientist Albert Einstein, written by his son, Einstein is described as spending several days trying to figure out what made the Drinking Duck work.

Chapter Sixteen

Albert, The Drinking Duck

If you were a child of the 1950's, surely the name Tigrett Toys would bring back memories of days gone by.

The man who created Tigrett Toys was John Burton Tigrett. He was born on September 29, 1913, in Jackson, Tennessee. When he was two, his parents separated, and he moved with his mother to Jackson, Mississippi, where she ran a Baptist Orphans' Home. Later, he was taken in by his uncle, Isaac Tigrett, who would become president of the 2,900-mile Gulf, Mobile & Ohio and Alton railroads.

After attending the University of Tennessee, he set about

making a living as a book salesman, investment counselor, official of a nationwide bus company, hotel owner, author and Florida real estate investor. In the late 1940s, Tigrett was a freelance writer selling stories to Reader's Digest and The Saturday Evening Post.

On a Saturday morning in Washington, he noticed a six-inch glass tube with a bulb on one end covered with a small piece of toweling. It was attached to a glass of water with a little wire cradle made from a paper clip. The liquid would run up the tube, causing the head to dip into the water. This would break the seal, the water would run down, and the process would repeat itself.

The inventor was Charles Howard, a well-known concert violinist. He owned the patent for the invention but had sold half of his rights to a friend for $250. Tigrett purchased the patent rights for $1,600. After finding a specialty glassmaker to produce tubes, a stamped cradle was added that looked like legs, a duck bill, a funny hat and two crossed eyes on the top, and feathers and a little paint completed the costume. Named Albert for a close friend, the Drinking Duck was ready to market. As a test, Walgreens store windows in Chicago were rented for the weekend, at the corner of State and Randolph, often described as the busiest traffic corner in the United States. More than a thousand of the ducks were then placed behind the windows all bobbing up and down. When the store opened the next morning, such a large crowd gathered near the ducks that the police were called. All the ducks were quickly sold, making it one of the most successful toys of all time.

In a book about the famous scientist Albert Einstein, written by his son, Einstein is described as spending several days trying to figure out what made the Drinking Duck work. He never did! I often wonder how Charles Howard, the man who invented the duck, felt about the incredible success of the toy and the money he could have made.

With the success of the Drinking Duck, Tigrett began to look around for other toys he could develop and market. One day a man named Fritz Weigel called with a toy he invented. Fritz was head of research for a B.F. Goodrich Company division in Cleveland, Ohio. The invention was a small sprocket with five suction cups on it. By placing a small hole in the suction cup, it would release after a fraction of a second, and the next suction cup would take hold. This is what gave the appearance of the bird walking. The device was designed to be placed on a mirror or glass surface. But it could only go down. To make it go up, a stair and a spring were added, and Yogi Bird was ready for the market. Shortly thereafter, Fritz moved to Jackson as head of research for Tigrett Industries, which he also moved to Jackson and located in an old church building.

Fritz was profiled in Popular Mechanics with Yogi Bird which was in full production then and had earned Fritz more than half a million dollars!

Many toys would follow, some successful and some that were not. Another success was the Zoomaroy, a plastic paper on a stick, which, with the flick of a wrist, would shoot out five feet and then return. "Young gunfighters" could duel for hours without anyone getting hurt.

Charles and Rae Eames, a husband and wife architect team from Los Angeles, designed three toys that Tigrett Industries produced. One was called the House of Cards with striking photographs. Each card had slots in them that would enable you to build with them. The Giant House of Cards was a much larger version. The Tower was a building set of dowels and large sheets of tough paper.

With new products being tested, John Burton Tigrett came up with a unique way to test them. He used neighborhood children, nine or ten years old, who were invited to play with the toys. A driver picked the children up in a white 1950 Suburban with Tigrett Industries on the door and took them to the plant where they gave their opinions.

It was a magic time in Jackson with all the toys, especially if you were nine or ten years old. And Albert the Drinking Duck started it all!

There is little doubt that Ray Henry, the Game Warden, holds the record for the amount of anti-venom he received after dealing with rattlesnakes, copperheads and cottonmouths!

Chapter Seventeen

The Game Warden

I once had a friend named Ray Henry. He was a big man -- a really big man. But it was not because he was tall or heavy or wide. If he was not really that large, why would I think or say he was a big man. Perhaps it was because of his hands. They were large and calloused from work outside. If he thumped you on the back, you knew how big his hands were. But the biggest part of Ray Henry, a part I will always remember, was his smile. A smile, a mischievous smile, one that was always saying, "Let's go do something fun."

The first time I met Ray should have been an omen of

things to come. And of course, we were in the Hatchie Bottoms. A good friend, who was a game warden, introduced me to Ray. He indicated he was moving toward retirement as a game warden. He was looking for territory that needed beaver control. Our farm was beginning to have a significant population, so I suggested we take a look. One area was muddy, and I was concerned about getting stuck. Ray, however, thought it would not be a problem. We got stuck, really stuck! And the only way back was to walk through the mud and cross a large slough with water up to our waist. It was the beginning of an emerging friendship.

Through the years, Ray rarely talked about his experiences as a game warden in East Tennessee. However, if you listened carefully, stories began to emerge. In the 1963 summer edition of Southern Outdoors, there is an article about Ray and a wild boar named Satan who lived in the 199,000 acre Brimstone Creek Watershed near Crossville, Tennessee. Ray was one of the individuals involved in catching the wild hogs and moving them to another area. Only ropes and dogs were used. In Ray's first encounter with Satan, the hog killed one of Ray's dogs and crippled another. Ray escaped by climbing up a tree. Two years later Ray had another encounter with Satan. Again the monster killed two of Ray's dogs before he was able to tie him up. After looking at all of the scars on the old hog, a testament to years of combat, Ray took pity and released him, saying, "Satan is King again."

Five years later in June 1968, Ray was in the news again. An article and pictures of Ray appeared in the Roane County News. This time it was a bear rather than a wild hog. The article described a large black bear that had climbed a tree in a residential neighborhood after leaving the Catoosa Wildlife Area. After the bear received a tranquilizer shot, Ray took off his shirt and shoes, climbed up the tree, and tied a rope around the bear's foot by which he could be pulled out of the tree.

When Ray moved back to West Tennessee, there were no resident bears or wild hogs, but he found lots of cottonmouths and copperhead snakes to catch. And he loved to play with them. One day he caught an unusually large cottonmouth that he had been watching for some time. He placed the snake in a burlap bag and started out of the swamp. When he slipped down and released his grip on the bag, the snake slipped out and struck Ray in the chest. Fortunately Ray was wearing canvas clothing which the snake could not puncture. But he would not let go. Ray told me he held the snake until he thought his arm would fall off before finally getting the snake back in the bag.

Several years later, Ray was breaking up a beaver dam in the Hatchie Bottoms when he was struck by a cottonmouth. This put him in the hospital for several days where he received a number of anti-venom shots. Even though he recovered, it had been dangerous. Yet many people are bitten, and most all of them survive. But Ray was not the average person. His interest in snakes continued, and he kept several large snakes in a box to show people. And once again he was bitten by a large rattlesnake. This time the situation was even worse than before, and for a time, there was concern whether the bite would be fatal. There is little doubt that Ray holds the record for the amount of anti-venom he received.

Over the years, I have seen very few poisonous snakes. Perhaps it was because I tried not to look for them. On one occasion, I was moving boards for a duck blind in the Forked Deer River bottoms. It was swampy ground with lots of brush. I did not even see a snake. When I told Ray about it, he replied, "I wonder how many saw you!"

For more than twenty years, Ray and I hunted for Indian arrowheads with my two boys in the Forked Deer and Hatchie bottoms. Ray was more like a father than a friend to my children. We carried sardines, crackers and potted meat for lunch and "belly washers," Ray's term for a Coke, or peach soda to wash them down.

As time moved on, my boys grew up, and Ray and I got older. As farmers moved to no-till planting and no longer plowed the ground, our days of finding arrowheads came to an end. One day I asked my boys about their favorite memory of our days with Ray. They remembered an afternoon in the Hatchie Bottoms when Ray and both boys were having a great day with numerous finds. I could find not a thing until I found a large turtle about the size of two basketballs. After picking him up, I went to where Ray and the boys were, only to find them doubled over with laughter. The turtle, perhaps to express his displeasure at being picked up, was going to the bathroom soaking my shirt. It was a day they never forgot.

As time went on, we seemed to take different paths and saw less of each other. Ray grew ill, and one day he was gone. He had been a big part of our lives, a part we could not replace. We often think of Ray and his big smile, and I still see his face and hear his laughter when I think of the day I found the big turtle.

Looking Back... Henderson used to be the second largest town in Madison County before Chester County was formed.

When Casey Jones had his wreck on April 30, 1900, his firemen was Sim Webb. When the wreck occurred, Casey's last words were "Jump, Sim." Sim survived the crash through battered and bruised. For his injuries, the Illinois Central railroad awarded him "five dollars."

Steve Fossett was well-known for his world records and adventures as a balloonist and with his success with sailboats, gliders, and powered aircraft.

Chapter Eighteen

The Man Who Flew Around the World

Steve Fossett was born in Jackson, Tennessee in April 1944 but grew up in Garden City, California. His interest in adventure began at an early age. Not gifted in athletics, he followed in the footsteps of his father, an Eagle Scout. By his thirteenth birthday, he too became an Eagle Scout. Fossett would say that Scouting was the most important activity of his youth. When he was twelve, he began climbing the mountains of California, starting with the San Jacinto Range.

After graduating from Stanford, he spent the summer

climbing mountains and swimming in the Dardanelles, a strait of water in northwest Turkey. Next came graduate school at Washington University in St. Louis, where he earned a master's degree and then entered the business world earning millions of dollars as a commodity trader and as the founder of Marathon Securities and Lakota Trading. His success in the business world enabled him to travel and live a life of adventure.

Fossett was well-known for his world records and adventures as a balloonist and with his success with sailboats, gliders, and powered aircraft. An experienced aviator, he became the first person to create a new world record, flying around the world in a balloon solo and nonstop from Western Australia and returning fourteen days later. The gondola from his ten-story-high balloon, The Spirit of Freedom, was placed on display at the Smithsonian Museum. (This may remind you of the English daredevil Phileas Fogg in the movie *Around the World in 80 Days.*)

Fossett was one of the world's most accomplished sailors, speed sailing was his specialty. From 1993 to 2004, he set twenty-three world records and nine distance race records, sailing around the world in fifty-eight days in 2007. In 2004, he set the world speed record for airships (dirigibles). Between February 28 and March 3, Fossett made the first solo nonstop flight around the world at an average speed of 342.2 miles per hour. The team of Steve Fossett and Terry Delore of New Zealand set ten world records in gliders flying from Argentina, Nevada and New Zealand.

Among other things, Fossett was one of the first participants in the Worldloppet, a series of cross-country ski marathons around the world. He was one of the first skiers to compete in all ten of the long distance races. He also set a world record in Colorado skiing from Aspen to Vail in fifty-nine hours.

A lifelong mountain climber, Fossett climbed the highest peaks on six of the seven continents. After training for five years, he competed in the Iditarod Trail Sled Dog Race in Alaska finishing forty-seventh. In September 1985, he became the forty-seventh person to swim the English Channel. As a runner he competed in the Ironman Triathlon in Hawaii, the Boston Marathon, and the Leadville Trail 100, where he ran up elevations 14,000 feet in the Rocky Mountains. He competed in 1970 and again twenty years later in 1990.

On September 3, 2007, Fossett took off in a small plane from a private airstrip in Nevada near the California border and was not heard from again. The search for Fossett and his plane continued for the next thirty days. On October 2, the Civil Air Patrol announced that it had called off the search.

The Nevada search cost $1.6 million, the largest search and rescue mission ever conducted for an individual in the United States. (This would be Fossett's last world record!) His wrecked plane and skeleton remains were not found until a year later by a hiker in the Ansel Adams Wilderness Area, about sixty-five miles from the take-off site.

During his lifetime, Fossett set 116 world records. At the time of his death, sixty of these records were still standing. But no matter how many of them are broken, it is unlikely that anyone will ever achieve as many world records as Steve Fossett.

Looking Back... Alexander Blackburn Bradford was one of the first settlers in Madison County. Small in stature but extremely brave, he was a general in the war with Mexico. He is buried in Holly Springs, Mississippi, but his wife is buried in Jackson at Riverside Cemetery.

Lieutenant Wiley Hale and Lieutenant Thomas Ewell were killed at the Battle of Cerro Gordo in the war with Mexico in 1847. They are buried at historic Riverside Cemetery.

After doing a show in Parkin, Arkansas, with Johnny Cash and Elvis, Carl Perkins witnessed someone on the dance floor saying, "Stay off my new suede shoes." Carl wrote the song, and Sun Records released it on January 1, 1955.

Chapter Nineteen

The Music Men

Music has always been a big part of life in West Tennessee. Sitting on Interstate 40, the Music Highway between Nashville and Memphis, guitars, banjos and fiddles are playing louder than ever. Three individuals stand out as having a major influence on the music industry. One of them is Eddy Arnold, and two others are Carl Perkins and Sonny Boy Williamson.

Eddy Arnold

Eddy Arnold grew up on a farm near Henderson and went to school in Pinson. His father was a sharecropper who played a fiddle, and his mother played a guitar. Starting as a young boy, he played both the guitar and banjo. With the need to help with work on the farm, he left school before he could graduate. Even so, he continued performing with his guitar. Local legend has him coming to events, riding on a mule with his guitar on his back.

His music career began when he was sixteen years old, singing in Jackson on radio station WTJS. Within a year, he was working for the station and performing at local nightclubs using the nickname the Tennessee Plowboy. For the next several years, he continued to perform for radio stations, first in Memphis, then in St. Louis, Missouri, and Louisville, Kentucky.

In 1943, he made his debut performance on the Grand Ole Opry and a year later signed a contract with RCA Victor. His manager was Colonel Tom Parker, who later managed Elvis Presley. Arnold's second song to be released, "Each Minute Seems a Million Years," moved to No. 5 on the country charts, and he was on his way. His next fifty-seven songs all scored in the top ten including nineteen of them that finished number one on the country charts.

With the rise in popularity of rock and roll in the 1950s, sales declined. Arnold and Jim Reeves began using orchestras in the background, and they created a new sound that appealed to a more diverse audience. The new style became known as the "Nashville Sound."

In 1965, his song "What's He Doing In My World" reached number one on the charts. Six months later, he recorded "Make the World Go Away," with Floyd Cramer on the piano. It would become an international success. In the late 1960s, he performed with symphony orchestras in New York, Las Vegas and Hollywood, doing two concerts at Carnegie Hall and one at the Coconut Grove in Las Vegas.

In 1966, he was inducted into the Country Music Hall of Fame, the youngest performer to receive this honor. The following year, he was the first ever to receive the Country Music Association's Entertainer of the Year honor. Two years after receiving this award, he released his autobiography, *It's a Long Way From Chester County.*

By 1992 he had sold nearly 85 million records and had 135 weeks of No. 1 songs, more than any other singer. As the title of his book says, the Tennessee Plowboy had indeed come a long way from Chester County!

Carl Perkins

Carl Perkins grew up poor. The son of a sharecropper family, he was born near Tiptonville in Lake County. As a child, he listened to Southern gospel music in church and

African-American music sung in the fields of cotton around him. That music from the fields and churches would stay with him and influence the rest of his life.

But at first, the Perkins family was poor, and life was tough. One day on a rabbit hunt in Hatchie Bottoms, Carl told me about growing up and his first shotgun. The gun was an old single shot used to hunt rabbits.

"I only had two or three shells in my pockets, and I was hunting for supper, not for sport," he said.

After listening to Roy Acuff and the Grand Ole Opry, Carl began dreaming about playing the guitar, but the family was unable to buy one. His father, Buck, made one for him out of a cigar box and a broomstick. It didn't play music, but it let him pretend. A year later, a neighbor going through hard times sold a scratched-up Gene Autry model to Buck Perkins who gave it to his son.

When Carl was fourteen, the family moved, first to Bemis and then to Jackson. Using Roy Acuff and Bill Monroe as models, he continued to teach himself to play the guitar. When Carl and his brother began playing at the Cotton Boll, Carl received his first paycheck. He was not yet fifteen and on his way. Other jobs followed, and another brother, Clayton, joined the group as bass player. When W.S. Holland joined as a drummer, the group was complete. By 1953, they were playing in nightclubs and taverns six nights a week.

In January 1955 Carl signed a contract with Flip Records, a subsidiary of Sun Records in Memphis. His first release, "Movie Magg," started slowly. However, he was able to secure bookings where he opened with Elvis Presley following him. After doing a show in Parkin, Arkansas, with Johnny Cash and Elvis, he witnessed someone on the dance floor saying, "Stay off my new suede shoes." Carl wrote the song, and Sun Records released it on January 1, 1955.

"Blue Suede Shoes" put twenty-three-year-old Carl Perkins in the national spotlight. He was soon offered a chance to be on the Ed Sullivan and Perry Como shows, but he was involved in a terrible wreck in Delaware on the way to New York and sustained a fractured skull and a broken arm. This seemed to slow Carl's momentum in pop music, though his place in music history was assured.

Carl continued to write songs, always staying with the pure rockabilly style. The Beatles recorded three of his songs, with Paul McCartney saying, "If there were no Carl Perkins, there would be no Beatles." In 1965, he joined Johnny Cash's road show, playing guitar and singing for the next ten years. His last major concert was the Music for Montserrat All-Star Concert for charity at London's Royal Albert Hall on September 15, 1977.

A strong advocate for the prevention of child abuse, Carl worked with the Jackson Exchange Club to establish the first center for the prevention of child abuse in Tennessee and the fourth in the nation.

He was inducted into the Rock and Roll Hall of Fame in 1987. Today the Carl Perkins Center for the Prevention of Child Abuse, as well as his rockabilly music, serves as a reminder and a monument to his life in Madison County.

John Lee Curtis, "Sonny Boy" Williamson

"Sonny Boy" Williamson was born in Madison County near Jackson in 1914. He was a blues harmonica player, singer and songwriter. While still a teenager, he joined Yank Rachell and Sleepy John Estes playing with them in Tennessee and Arkansas. He picked up the name Sonny Boy because he was only sixteen when he began to follow the Mississippi River north with his harmonica hoping to make a living.

By the time he was in his late teens, he was established as a musician playing what was called "country blues." When he was twenty, he lived in Chicago. A self-taught music star, he began recording for Bluebird Records in 1937, singing and playing harmonica. His first song, "Good Morning Little Schoolgirl," was an instant hit. Over the next ten years, he released more than 120 new recordings. His style and his voice were instantly recognizable due to his slight voice impediment. His name spread like wildfire in the music world, and he was unquestionably the most influential harmonica player of his generation.

In 1947, his song "Shake the Boogie" was a nationwide hit. He was only thirty-four, but at the top of his career. A year later, in June 1948, he was returning from a recording session on Chicago's South Side when he was robbed, beaten and stabbed to death with an ice pick. His last words were reported to be "Lord have mercy."

In 1980 he was inducted into the Blues Foundation Hall of Fame. He is buried at the former Blair's Chapel Church southwest of Jackson. A red granite marker placed on the gravesite often holds harmonicas left by fans who visit the spot. Dozens of people and bands have performed in Jackson and West Tennessee, but Eddy Arnold, Carl Perkins, and Sonny Boy Williamson are at the top of the list.

Looking Back... Emma Inman Williams was the first Madison County historian. In 1946, she published *Historic Madison: The Story of Jackson and Madison County, Tennessee From the Prehistoric Moundbuilders to 1917.*

Legend has it that the young James Merriwether married Molly just before he left for war and died a short while later in a prison camp. But they had a son, who one day met his irascible grandfather and said he would prove he was his grandson.

Chapter Twenty

The Family Tree

This is a story about old Denmark, Tennessee, and a story of a young soldier. The story has two endings or perhaps three! You will have to choose which one you like best.

December 1861 was a time of patriotic speeches, of flags and banners. And it was a time of soldiers going off to war when this story began.

There was little war news as the year crept to an end. Soldiers from both armies stayed close to their winter camps as the weather grew colder. It had been seven months since

Company K, the Denmark Danes of the 6th Tennessee Infantry, had marched away from the front of the Denmark Presbyterian Church. And still, the South needed more soldiers for the battles that would surely come by springtime.

The 51st Tennessee Infantry Regiment was organized on January 1, 1862. All of the men were from West Tennessee. Four of the eight companies were composed of men from Madison County.

Joseph Merriwether was only seventeen when he rode away. Against his parents' wishes, he joined men from Denmark and Jackson as a private in Company D of the 51st Tennessee Infantry. The regiment went into camp at Henderson Station in Madison County (now Chester County). The unit remained in camp there until January 28. They were poorly trained and did not have weapons when they received orders to proceed to Danville to guard bridges across the Tennessee River.

From Danville, the 51st moved to Fort Henry where they were given inefficient double-barreled shotguns to defend the fort against Federal gunboats. Because of high water, the unit was moved once again, this time to Fort Donelson. The regiment was placed on the left of the Confederate line in support of an artillery battery. On February 16, the Southern forces surrendered. Over 2,000 Confederate soldiers were sent to Camp Butler, Illinois. Joseph Merriwether was one of the prisoners.

During the Civil War, Camp Butler was the second largest training camp in Illinois. It was quickly pressed into service as a prison to house 2,000 Confederate prisoners who had been captured at Fort Donelson.

The camp was poorly constructed out of boards and tar paper. Living conditions were miserable. Food was scarce with a biscuit and a cup of coffee, food for a day. Overcrowding and extreme weather quickly led to outbreaks of disease and death. Prisoners started dying almost immediately. In less than a month, 148 prisoners were buried in a Confederate cemetery. Over 700 Confederate soldiers died in 1862 of smallpox and other diseases.

On March 3, 1862, Joseph Merriwether died. He was only eighteen years old and had been a Confederate soldier for just over two months. He is buried in Camp Butler National Cemetery, one of 866 Confederate soldiers buried there. Alongside them are the graves of 776 Union soldiers. It is easy to distinguish the Confederate tombstones as they have a pointed headstone, which, according to superstition, keeps the devil from sitting on them!

This should be the end of the story. However, rather than the end, it is only the beginning. The balance of the story comes from Fonville Neville, often called the "poet laureate of Denmark." In addition to being a rural mail carrier, Fonville wrote a column for the *Jackson Sun* and *Memphis Press-Scimitar*. His stories bring back the years when Denmark was in its prime. They were written under the caption "Along Rural By-Paths." Thanks to Fonville, here is the rest of the story of Private Joseph Merriwether.

The Merriwethers were considered to be the "blue bloods" of Denmark. Extensive landowners, the family lived in a large house on a hill near the Methodist Cemetery. Joseph was the son of Francis "Samuel" Merriwether and Louisa "Lizzie" Merriwether. Fonville describes Francis as being cold and stern.

In the weeks before he was to leave, Joseph fell deeply in love with a young woman, Molly (or Mary) Womack. When Joseph's father became aware of the romance, he sternly forbade them to marry and threatened to disinherit his son if he did so. Despite this warning, on the night before he left, Joseph and Molly were married by the regimental chaplain. Two fellow soldiers served as witnesses. Keeping the marriage a secret, Joseph hid the marriage certificate in a book in the family library.

Just over two months later, Joseph died, far away in a Yankee prison. The chaplain and the two soldiers who witnessed the wedding were killed in battle. Somehow word reached Denmark that Joseph had been captured. This information is contained in a family diary. It is unlikely that they were aware of his death, however.

And now, the story gets complicated. Molly was pregnant and soon gave birth to a baby boy. When Molly carried the baby to Joseph's father, he laughed at her, asking if there were witnesses at the wedding, and where the preacher and the marriage certificate were. Since Molly had none of these, the old man told them to go and not come back.

It would be eight years before Molly told her son who his father was and who his grandfather was. When her son learned this, he went to see his grandfather. He found Francis dozing in a chair, by now growing old and feeble. When the young boy confronted his grandfather, the boy received the same bitter reception as his mother had received when he was born. Joseph told him, "I'll get my rights because there's a God in heaven" to which the old man replied, "Perhaps so, but He don't practice in the courts down here!"

A year later, the old man was dead. On the night he was buried, Joseph's son dreamed he was in the Merriwether home. A voice told him there was a paper in a book, and he must go and look for it. When Molly and Joseph attended the reading of the will, they found a codicil had been added, saying if Molly could provide proof of the marriage, her son would receive the entire estate. Remembering the dream, the boy walked to the bookcase, selected a book, and when he opened it, a marriage certificate fell out! Thus, the nine-year-old son of Joseph Merriwether inherited the house on the hill and all of the Merriwether estate.

Did it really happen that way? I can tell you that Joseph did serve in the 51st Tennessee Infantry, was captured and died and is buried at Camp Butler. All of the old stories say he did marry Molly (or Mary) the night before he left and was the father of their son. How do you think they discovered the marriage certificate? I told you what Fonville Neville said. Perhaps you can make a better ending.

Of the 100 or more people who live in Denmark, there are no Merriwethers. On a nearby hill, bits of pottery and bricks are the only reminders of their home. And yet, if you can close your eyes for a moment, you can see an eight-year-old boy on his way to confront his grandfather.

Looking Back... Denmark once rivaled Jackson in size and prominence. A series of fires and failure of the railroad to come through caused its demise. Today less than a dozen people live there.

Jackson's most famous outlaw was John H. Murrell. Adept at stealing horses and slaves, his gang operated in eight states. His home was near Denmark where treasure hunters still look for buried gold.

In many ways, La Grange has changed little since the years before the Civil War when many of its historic homes were built. Woodlawn Plantation and Hancock Hall are two of the largest and most striking of the twenty or so antebellum homes.

Chapter Twenty-One

La Belle Village

La Grange, Tennessee, often called La Belle Village, or "beautiful village" is the oldest town in Fayette County. It is situated on a high bluff overlooking the Wolf River, only three miles from the Mississippi state line. Memphis is fifty miles to the west and Holly Springs is twenty-three miles south. Originally a Chickasaw Indian village and trading post, a post office was established there in 1828, and the town was chartered one year later.

If you look at the website for the Town of La Grange, Tennessee, you find this quote: "Few places exist today where your thoughts might take you on a leisurely stroll back in time and yet when you open your eyes the past remains. Imagine a sultry summer evening when you happen by a stately antebellum mansion, its long veranda nestled in the shade of a towering magnolia tree, beckoning you into its cool depths. And while you sit pondering the mysteries and stories the walls around you hold, history's drama suddenly unfolds in vivid details before you.

"You hear the lonesome sound of a train whistle in the distance, and the jingle of booted spurs, as a group of blue-clad soldiers hurry away into the night on some secret mission. You dare not speak for fear of waking up the hands of time, for you have found La Grange, Tennessee, where time has seemingly stood still."

At the onset of the Civil War, La Grange was a thriving community of more than 2,000 inhabitants. Today, though the little town is as beautiful as ever, its population is only 133.

A fire destroyed a portion of the town in 1873. Five years later, forty people died of yellow fever out of a population of only 320 people. In 1900, a tornado destroyed much of the business district and the Baptist, Methodist and Presbyterian churches.

The Civil War arrived in La Grange on June 13, 1862, less than one week after the fall of Memphis to Union troops. From that time, until the end of the war in 1865, La Grange would be occupied by Confederate or Union troops. Over sixty engagements, skirmishes and raids took place in or around it. More than forty houses and structures were burned or torn down by Federal soldiers to provide firewood. The new Presbyterian College was used as a prison and hospital before being torn down to provide bricks for fireplaces for Union soldiers. In 1862, prior to the advance on Vicksburg, 30,000 Union troops were camped in or around the town. One of the camps occupied eighty acres of the historic Immanuel Episcopal Church, which was used as a hospital. The church pews and chancel furniture were used to make coffins for the Union dead.

Perhaps the most prominent part of La Grange's Civil War history centers around a Union cavalry raid led by Colonel Benjamin Grierson. On April 17, 1863, Grierson and 1,700 mounted cavalry left La Grange and headed south through the heart of the Confederacy. In many ways, Grierson was an unlikely commander to lead such an expedition. A thirty-seven-year-old music teacher, his only military service prior to the war was as a trumpet player in the Ohio militia. To complicate things, he had a deep distrust of horses. As a child, he had been kicked in the face, causing a wound that left a long scar on his cheek. Consequently, he wore a full beard to cover it.

The troops, composed of 6th and 7th Illinois and the 2nd Iowa

Cavalry, covered 600 miles in sixteen days, ending up in Union-held Baton Rouge, Louisiana. They captured 500 Confederates and killed or wounded a hundred more. They destroyed fifty miles of railroad tracks and telegraph lines and captured 1,000 mules and horses, 3,000 rifles and lost only thirty-six men. The raid had been a huge success in that it diverted large numbers of Confederate troops which left Grant and General William T. Sherman free to concentrate on the capture of Vicksburg, Mississippi. As a result of the raid, Grierson was promoted to brigadier general. By the end of the war, he had risen to the rank of major general. It was quite a career for a soldier who, at the beginning of the war, was a trumpet player in a militia unit! In 1958 John Wayne and William Holden co-starred in the movie *The Horse Soldiers* based on Grierson's raid.

In many ways, La Grange has changed little since the years before the Civil War when many of its historic homes were built. Woodlawn Plantation and Hancock Hall are two of the largest and most striking of the twenty or so antebellum homes. Woodlawn Plantation, built in 1828, sits high on a hill overlooking the town. In 1862, it was used as a Union hospital and as the headquarters for Sherman. Hancock Hall, built nearly thirty years later, was the headquarters of General Stephen Hurlbut. Union soldiers camped in its back yard.

Perhaps someday La Grange will begin to grow again to what it was before the Civil War. Perhaps not. Though smaller, it retains all of the beauty and charm of long ago. In many ways, I hope it never changes.

Looking Back... In 1926, Jennings Perry of Jackson wrote *The Windy Hill.* The book, though fiction, describes a real lady in Jackson, Clay Long, who dances in the moonlight with very little clothing.

Randolph is sixty miles upriver from Memphis. It once had the opportunity to become the largest city in Tennessee. Today less than fifty people live there.

On the night of April 27, 1865, the Sultana, a sidewheeler paddle boat was nine miles north of Memphis when it blew up. With 2,400 passengers on board, more than 1,800 people lost their lives. It is the greatest maritime disaster in American history.

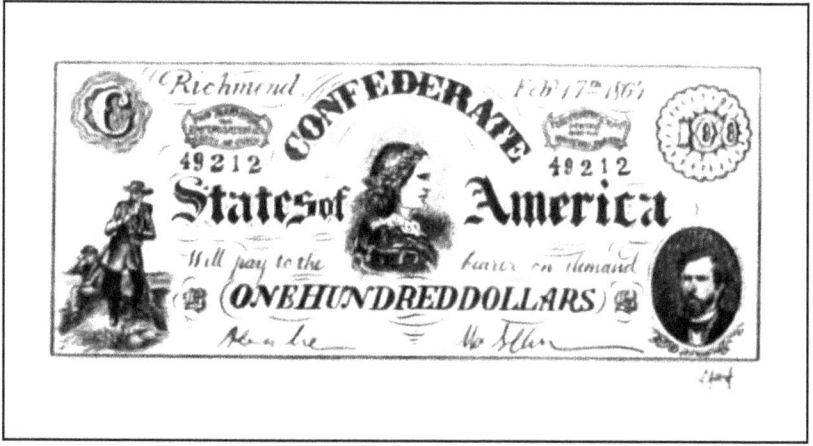

With her knowledge of French and Russian and with her elaborate wardrobe, Lucy Pickens soon became a court favorite of Czar Alexander II and Czarina Maria in St. Petersburg.

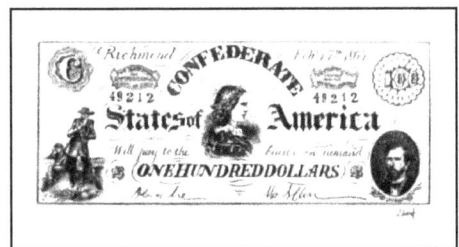

Chapter Twenty-Two

Sweetheart of the Confederacy

Lucy Petway Holcombe was born on the family plantation near La Grange, Tennessee, in June 1832. She grew up in the beautiful little village of La Grange and was a student at La Grange Female Academy. When she was fourteen, she was sent away to a finishing school for young women in Bethlehem, Pennsylvania. In 1845, the Holcombe family moved to Marshall, Texas. They would never return to live in West Tennessee, except for summer vacations.

As a young woman, Lucy was described as "beautiful, brilliant and captivating" by the men who courted her.

Though she was sought by many suitors, she remained single until the summer of 1857 when she was courted by Francis Wilkinson Pickens, a prominent South Carolina politician. Born in 1805, he was twenty-seven years older than Lucy and twice widowed. At first, Lucy took little interest in him until he was offered the position of minister to Russia by President James K. Polk. This apparently changed her mind, and they were married soon after.

With her knowledge of French and Russian and with her elaborate wardrobe, she soon became a court favorite of Czar Alexander II and Czarina Maria in St. Petersburg. The czar and his wife showered Lucy with gifts and ultimately became godparents of the Pickenses' daughter Eugenia who was born while they were in Russia.

As the South moved toward secession, the Pickenses returned home. In August 1860, Francis Pickens was elected governor of South Carolina, three days before South Carolina seceded from the Union. On January 9, 1861, Governor Pickens sanctioned the firing by The Citadel cadets on a steamship, The Star of the West, that was attempting to bring supplies to the Union garrison at Fort Sumter. These were the first shots fired in the Civil War. When the attack on Fort Sumter began on April 1, Lucy and a group of friends watched the bombardment from a nearby rooftop.

Considered by many to be the most beautiful woman in the Confederacy, her image was placed on three issues of the Confederate $100 bill and on one issue of the $1 bill. She was the only woman whose likeness was ever placed on Confederate currency. One unit of the Confederate army, the Holcombe Legion, was named for her. It was rumored that she sold some of the jewelry given to her by Czar Alexander to pay for outfitting the unit.

At the end of the Civil War, a constitutional convention was called to rejoin the Union. Francis Pickens was quoted as saying, "It doesn't become South Carolina to vapor or swell or strut or brag or bluster or threat or swagger.... She bids us bind up her wounds and pour on the oil of peace."

Francis Pickens died four years later at the age of sixty-three. Lucy Pickens lived for another thirty years, managing the family plantations in Edgefield, South Carolina. She never returned to her home in La Grange.

Today, her childhood home, Westover of Woodstock, is as beautiful as it was long before the Civil War. A Tennessee historical marker sits near the house. In the springtime when the flowers are in bloom, it seems as if the old homeplace is calling for "The Queen of the Confederacy" to return .

Looking Back... There were more casualties at Shiloh than the combined numbers of all previous American wars!

Joe W. Rogers Sr. set the concept of a fast-food chain, dine-in restaurant that would be open twenty-four hours a day, 365 days a year. The restaurant was named after the most profitable item on the sixteen-item menu. The fragile nature of waffles also made the point that it was a dine-in, not a carryout restaurant.

Chapter Twenty-Three

The Waffle King

Few people know that American businessman Joe W. Rogers Sr., known to many people as the co-founder and CEO of Waffle House, grew up in Jackson, Tennessee.

Born in December 1919, his family lived at 291 West Deaderick Street. It was a world with no car, radio, television, newspaper and very little money, but a world of close-knit families and neighborhoods.

As Joe put it, "We weren't poor, we just didn't have any money."

When the stock market crashed in October 1929, the next

ten years would be known as "The Great Depression." Jackson suffered the Great Depression just as much as other cities did. As the railroads slowed down, Joe's father was laid off but soon found a job delivering laundry. In Joe's words, "We didn't have a lot of money, but nobody much was rich in Jackson."

Joe was an Eagle Scout, but like other boys, he never had a uniform. In high school, he was tall for his age and played football for the Golden Bears under Coach Tury Oman who had a simple motto: "We don't lose!"

After high school, Joe was offered a football scholarship at Union University; however, despite the offer, the family could not afford the balance of tuition, and Joe went to work for S.H. Kress, the dime store, for seven dollars a week. Kress was located in downtown Jackson on North Liberty Street adjacent to Woolworth's. Kress is now Kmart. It was at Kress that Joe learned this principle: "You never lose a satisfied customer." It was a business lesson he never forgot.

As America began to recover from the Depression in 1940, the railroads began running again, and Joe's father went back to work for the railroad. This enabled Joe to give up his job at Kress. Instead of returning to Union University, he elected to join the 117th Infantry Division at $60 a month, twice what he was making at Kress, and the military fed and clothed him.

Soon after this, he transferred to the Air Corps and by 1945 and the end of World War II, he was a four-engine B-24 instructor.

After his discharge, he accepted a job offer from Fred Smith to work in the Toddle House restaurant chain. He started in 1947 as a short order cook at the Toddle House in New Haven, Connecticut. By 1949, he had become a regional manager for the company and had moved to Atlanta where he bought a house from a Realtor named Tom Forkner. They would become best friends and business partners.

Rogers, inspired by the rapid growth of chains like McDonalds, proposed that he and Forkner form a partnership and build a small, quick-service sit-down restaurant. Rogers told Forkner, "You build a restaurant, and I'll show you how to run it." After choosing a site, the pair worked together, with Forkner selecting the name Waffle House, and Rogers set the concept of a fast-food chain, dine-in restaurant that would be open twenty-four hours a day, 365 days a year.

The restaurant was named after the most profitable item on the sixteen-item menu. The fragile nature of waffles also made the point that it was a dine-in, not a carryout restaurant. As Americans began eating out more, the little store started well and continued to prosper.

Rogers continued to work with Toddle House and to avoid a

conflict of interest, sold his interest to his partner Forkner. Four years later, Rogers tried to buy into Toddle House but was refused. So he left Toddle House and became full-time manager of restaurant operations for Waffle House.

After opening its fourth restaurant in 1960, Waffle House began franchising restaurants and had twenty-seven stores by the late 1960s.

As of 2013, the company had over 2,500 locations in twenty-seven states. The original founders, Rogers and Forkner, continue to own a majority of the business. In many ways, the menu of today is similar to the menu of the Waffle House of 1955. As always, the signature entrees are waffles with a single waffle priced at just under $3. There are seven waffle choices, eleven side orders, nine choices for eggs or omelets and eight ways to order a steak, chicken or pork chop. Much has changed since 1955, but much is the same as it has been for 60 years. Customer satisfaction is still the No. 1 priority.

The next time you pass a Waffle House, think of Joe W. Rogers, who grew up in Jackson and who lived here during the Depression era.

Looking Back... William Saunders, a mechanic in Canton, Mississippi, started the song that made Casey Jones famous. In 1909 it became a vaudeville hit. Soon versions of it were being sung throughout the country.

When James Dickey, the sheriff of McNairy County, was killed in an auto accident, Buford Pusser was elected to succeed him, becoming the youngest sheriff in Tennessee history.

Chapter Twenty-Four

Buford

I bet that you don't know who Jack and Louise Hathcock or Carl Douglas "Towhead" White were. Probably a good thing if you didn't as they were part of the infamous "State Line Mob" of the late 1950's and 1960's. The gambling, prostitution and murder they were a part of and the sheriff who sought to stop them is one of the most colorful stories of crime and law and order in West Tennessee history.

The name of the sheriff was Buford – Buford Hayse Pusser. He was the sheriff of McNairy County, and he carried a big stick. Buford was born in 1937 in the little town of Finger, not so far from Henderson. His father was the police chief of Adamsville.

Buford was a big man standing six feet six inches tall and weighing nearly 300 pounds. He towered over most of his contemporaries. A good athlete, he played high school basketball and football. Upon graduation, he entered the Marine Corps but was soon discharged due to asthma.

In 1957 Buford moved to Chicago where he was a professional wrestler known as "Buford the Bull." Five years later, he moved back to West Tennessee, accepting a job as police chief and constable of Adamsville. When James Dickey, the sheriff of McNairy County, was killed in an auto accident., Buford was elected to succeed him, becoming the youngest sheriff in Tennessee history.

Long known for its unsavory reputation and corruption, Buford began replacing the deputies and staff of the sheriff's department with men of his own choosing, including the first black deputy in the state of Tennessee (he was later murdered). Rather than using firearms to subdue criminals, Buford carried a four-foot long hickory stick, which became his trademark. He was elected on a platform of cleaning up McNairy County, which justifiably had the reputation as the most corrupt crime-ridden county in the state, if not the nation. Several organized crime gangs, based mainly in

Nashville, ran the criminal enterprises, which included gambling, prostitution, bootlegging (illegal whiskey sales), narcotics and automobile thefts.

The two main groups were "The Stateline Gang" and the "Dixie Mafia." In 1999, a Memphis newspaper reported that Buford jailed more than 7,500 criminals during his tenure as sheriff. In one year, he dismantled eighty-five illegal stills.

Part of my job in the 1960s was to work with banks in Adamsville and Savannah. One day at lunch, I was introduced to Buford who joined us. He told us of a large moonshine still he had discovered. When he first found it, there was no one at the site. Deciding to come back later, he started out of the woods when he heard a man returning to the still. Buford stepped behind a tree and a large black man walked right by him. As he did so, Buford stepped out and grabbed him saying, "Gotcha!" Startled and frightened, the man went to the bathroom, both on himself and Buford, too!

In 1970, Buford was ineligible for re-election due to the term limits then in effect. He was defeated in his bid to become sheriff again in 1972, but was later elected as a constable of Adamsville.

Two events are at the center of Pusser's years as sheriff of McNairy County. One was his gunfight with Louise Hathcock and the other was the ambush and murder of his wife Pauline.

The State Line Gang was a group of criminals who operated in the 1950s and 1960s on the Mississippi-Tennessee state line in Alcorn County, Mississippi and McNairy County, Tennessee. Among the motels or restaurants they operated was the Shamrock Motel and Restaurant two miles north of Corinth off U.S. Highway 45. Louise Hathcock and her husband Jack were the owners. It specialized in gambling, illegal whiskey, moonshine whiskey, prostitution and murder for hire.

On February 1, 1966, Pusser went to the Shamrock to investigate a robbery complaint. When he entered the site, Louise Hathcock fired a shot at Pusser but missed. Buford then returned fire, killing her. (There are many stories about who shot first!)

Eighteen months later, Pusser received an early morning call about a disturbance on rural New Hope Road in McNairy County. His wife Pauline elected to ride with him. As they passed the New Hope Methodist Church, a car pulled alongside and opened fire, killing Pauline and hitting Buford in the face. Pusser identified four of the assassins, though they were not charged. Three of the four were killed in the following months by unknown assassins. The murder of Pauline Pusser brought national attention on Buford and his "war on the State Line Gang."

On August 21, 1974, Buford Pusser was killed in a one-car accident when he lost control of his car. Many believe the steering mechanism on the car had been sabotaged, leading to his death. Buford had survived seven stabbings and eight shootings, but met his death on the highway.

There have been five books about Buford and a movie *Walking Tall* in 1973. There have been two sequels to the movies, a movie made for television and a TV series. The Buford Pusser Home and Museum still exists in Adamsville as a reminder of the young lawman with the big stick. The Shamrock Motel no longer exists, and most of the members of the "State Line Gang" are but memories.

Looking Back... Fielding Hurst, a Yankee Colonel from McNairy County, held Jackson up for ransom in 1864. Even though the ransom was paid, his soldiers burned most of downtown Jackson.

On the evening of October 11, 1809, Meriwether Lewis died either by suicide or murder seventy-three miles south of Nashville on the Natchez Trace Parkway. Lewis was the co-leader of the Lewis and Clark Expedition.

The U.S. military launched Operation Magic Carpet to get tens of thousands of soldiers in Europe and Asia home for Christmas. And in the United States, Operation Santa Claus was in place to process soldiers who were to be discharged, home for the holidays.

Chapter Twenty-Five

Merry Christmas 1945

It was almost Christmas. Just three more days and as always, the calendar and the clock seemed to stand still. Stockings were hung, and trees were decorated even though ornaments were scarce. Soon it would be time to watch for a sleigh pulled by reindeer. And at long last, it would be a Christmas without war, the first since 1938.

The U.S. military launched Operation Magic Carpet to get tens of thousands of soldiers in Europe and Asia home for Christmas. And in the United States, Operation Santa Claus was in place to process soldiers who were to be discharged, home for the holidays. And yet the joy of Christmas could do little to ease the sadness of families where soldiers had been left behind in places like Normandy and Bastogne, soldiers who would never come home.

In Washington, President Harry Truman declared a four-day holiday for federal employees, an event without precedent, and much of the nation followed suit. Fresh snow covered the ground and nearly a thousand people gathered on the South Lawn of the White House on Christmas Eve for the National Tree Lighting Ceremony, despite below-zero temperatures. President Truman set the tone for the season when he said, "This is the Christmas that a war-weary world has prayed for."

Jackson would not have a white Christmas despite a frigid temperature of 4 degrees on December 23. It was expected to warm up during the week with rain likely, but no snow. Christmas turkeys remained scarce across the country, and many people made do with "Murkeys," a concoction of sausage, meat, vegetables, and bread crumbs molded into the shape of a turkey. Stores in Jackson, however, advertised that turkeys were available for Christmas at A&P Grocery. Turkeys were 52 cents a pound. If you wanted to save money, chickens were 46 cents a pound. For dessert, a fruitcake (three pounds) was only $1.65. Oranges were 59 cents a dozen, and oysters were 69 cents a pint. If you smoked (most Americans did smoke in 1945), cigarettes were a dollar six to a carton!

Piggly Wiggly did not offer turkey, but you could buy a Christmas tree for 59 cents, up to a $1.99 for a larger tree (Washington fir). Eggs were 65 cents a dozen and apples were 65 cents a pound. The Johnson cash grocery in Humboldt offered a pound of chocolates for 15 cents and a three-pound bag of coffee could be yours for 79 cents.

With only three shopping days left, some toys were featured in ads in The Jackson Sun. Firestone offered a steel play gym for $24.95. Frankland's had sleds for $7.95. And Holland's Toyland had scooters for $4.50 and toy fire trucks for $1.79. Santa's sled would be a little lighter this year, and it would be several years before many traditional toys would be available. However, children in Jackson and throughout America were much more fortunate than children in war-ravaged Europe, especially Germany.

For men, Kisber's had ties from $1 to $2.50. All leather slippers were $3.50. Tuchfeld's had "fuzzy wuzzy" gloves for $2.98. Robert's Jewelers offered a 10 percent discount for all service men and women, and Fenner Electric had sister coffee mugs for $2.95. Grand Leader advised shoppers they would be open until 9 p.m.

S.M. Lawrence Company advertised that "coal did the job." Beare Ice and Coal Company wanted people "to use more ice" and the National Bank of Commerce advised: "Use your extra dollars to buy U.S. War Bonds."

Though the "make-do mentality" of World War II would exist for some time, Jacksonians were beginning to be ready for Christmas cheer and entertainment. The Pit Restaurant on South Highland offered dancing and dining with bandleader Hal Strain. At the National Guard Armory, a "hayloft frolic and dance" was 60 cents a head. If you didn't have a car to get there, you could call City Taxi at 9235 or Stewart's Cab at 4909. Jackson had three movie theaters, the Paramount, The State and The Met. Bing Crosby starred in *East Side of Heaven* at the Paramount and also had the No. 1 record album, "Merry Christmas," which featured his recording of "White Christmas." There were special Christmas services at First Methodist and First Presbyterian.

The Christmas of 1945 was perhaps the best Christmas ever. There would be fewer presents that year, simpler decorations, and fewer celebrations and parties. But families were coming together as the soldiers returned home. The war was over, and the best present of all was that "good will toward men" was here again.

An ad in The Jackson Sun from Beare Ice and Coal expressed it best: "The miracles of Santa Claus – Santa Claus as real in spirit as any living soul – gladness in the eyes of little children – warmer handclasps and that undimmed star of promise – promise of continued peace on earth so long as good men live and understand and pray – Christmas again – Christmas forever."

Looking Back... In 1950, on the anniversary of Casey Jones' last run, a commemorative postal stamp was issued.

Adam Huntsman is buried in Salem Cemetery on Cotton Grove Road. It was Huntsman who defeated Davy Crockett and sent him to Texas and the Alamo.

William Hicks "Red" Jackson was a Confederate general. His brother Howell E. Jackson was a Supreme Court Justice, making the Jackson brothers one of Jackson's most distinguished families.

Bibliography

A Descendant of One of the First Settlers. *Old Times in West Tennessee.* W.C. Cheeney Printer and Publishers, Memphis, Tennessee 1873. Reprinted by Windmill Publications, Inc., Mt. Vernon, Indiana, 1991.

Alexander, Harbert, *Old Trails and Tales of Tennessee.* Favorite Recipes Press, Nashville, Tennessee 2004.

Alexander, Harbert, *Tales of Madison.* Hillsboro Press, 238 Seaboard Lane, Franklin, Tennessee 2002.

Barry, John M. *The Great Influenza.* The Penguin Group, 375 Hudson Street, New York, New York, 2004.

Bowling, Lewis. *Wallace Wade Championship Years at Alabama and Duke.* Carolina Academic Press. Durham, North Carolina. 2006.

Glines, Carroll V. *Roscoe Turner Aviation's Master Showman.* Smithsonian Institution Press, Washington and London, 1995.

Hawkins, Herman, M.D. *The Story of George Frederick Burgoyne Howard: The Holy Cheat.* The West Tennessee Historical Society Papers. No. XVI, 1962.

Lewis, Elizabeth Wittenmeyer. *Queen of the Confederacy: The Innocent Deceits of Lucy Holcombe Pickens.* University of North Texas Press. 2002.

Litt, Matthew. *Christmas 1945: The Greatest Celebration in American History.* History Publishing Company, Palisades,

New York. 2010.

McCann, Kevin D. *Jackson Diamonds. Professional Baseball in Jackson, Tennessee.* Three Star Press, 283 Murrell Road, Dickson, Tennessee, 1999.

McKinney, Tom C. *Jack Hinson's One-Man War: A Civil War Sniper.* Pelican Publishing Company. Gretna, Louisiana. 2012.

Parsons, H. Lynn, and Parsons, Jerry M. Showman. *Shooter: The Life and Times of Herb Parsons.* Taylor Publishing Company, Dallas, 2009.

Perkins, Carl, and McGee, David. *Go, Cat, Go: The Life and Times of Carl Perkins.* Hyperion, 114 Fifth Avenue, New York, New York, 1996.

Pitts, John A. *Personal and Professional Reminiscences of an Old Lawyer.* Southern Publishers, Inc., Kingsport, Tennessee 1930.

Rogers, Joe W. Sr. *Who's Looking Out for the Poor Old Cash Customer?* Looking Glass Books, 730 Sycamore Street, Decatur, Georgia, 2000.

Tigrett, John Burton. *Fair and Square: A Collection of Stories from a Lifetime Among Friends.* Spiridon Press, Inc. 1998.

About the author

Harbert Alexander Sr. graduated from Jackson High School in 1957. He earned a bachelor's degree from the Virginia Military Institute in 1961 and a graduate degree from Rutgers University.

He served as an artillery officer in Schweinfurt, West Germany, retiring from the army as a captain. He is a member of the Military Writers Society of America.

He was associated with Jackson National Bank for twenty-four years where he served as president of the bank and vice chairman of the holding company. He was appointed president and CEO of Union Planters Bank of Jackson in 1988.

In 1998, Alexander was promoted to the position of regional president for all of the West Tennessee and Arkansas Union Planters Banks. He retired from Union Planters on June 30, 2004. Following this, he joined the Bank of Jackson as chairman and chief executive officer serving in this position until 2010 and now serves on the board of directors.

He served as chairman on the board of Lambuth University, and was the past chairman of the Jackson

Energy Authority board and past chairman of the board of Jackson-Madison County General Hospital. He was named Jackson Exchange Club's "Man of the Year" in 1991.

Alexander is president of the Carnegie Center, was the Madison County historian for 23 years, and serves on the board of the Tennessee State Museum, appointed by Gov. Bill Haslam. Alexander is active in historic preservation in Tennessee and has been an amateur archaeologist for more than 50 years.

He is the author of four books. He is married to Nora Dancy Noe and has three children and three grandchildren.

Harbert Alexander Sr. and Happy, his beloved Boston terrier, who is usually in his lap.

www.ingramcontent.com/pod-product-compliance
Lightning Source LLC
Chambersburg PA
CBHW040802150426
42811CB00081B/2371/J